MY DREAM IS TO BE BOLD:
OUR WORK TO END PATRIARCHY

Published 2011 by Pambazuka Press,
an imprint of Fahamu
Cape Town, Dakar, Nairobi and Oxford
www.pambazukapress.org
www.fahamubooks.org
www.pambazuka.org

Fahamu, 2nd floor, 51 Cornmarket Street,
Oxford OX1 3HA, UK
Fahamu Kenya, PO Box 47158, 00100 GPO,
Nairobi, Kenya
Fahamu Senegal, 9 Cité Sonatel 2, POB 25021,
Dakar-Fann, Dakar, Senegal
Fahamu South Africa, c/o 19 Nerina Crescent,
Fish Hoek, 7975 Cape Town, South Africa

British Library Cataloguing in Publication Data
A catalogue record for this book is available
from the British Library

ISBN: 978-1-906387-91-4 paperback
ISBN: 978-1-906387-92-1 ebook – pdf

Copyediting: Vaun Cornell
Proofreading: Catherine Thompson
Design and layout: WE Designs
Cover illustration: Noel Franzen

Printed by National Printing Press, Bangalore, India

Through the voices of the peoples of Africa and the global South, Pambazuka Press and Pambazuka News disseminate analysis and debate on the struggle for freedom and justice.

Pambazuka Press – www.pambazukapress.org

 A Pan-African publisher of progressive books and DVDs on Africa and the global South that aim to stimulate discussion, analysis and engagement. Our publications address issues of human rights, social justice, advocacy, the politics of aid, development and international finance, women's rights, emerging powers and activism. They are primarily written by well-known African academics and activists. All books are available as ebooks.

Pambazuka News – www.pambazuka.org

 The award-winning and influential electronic weekly newsletter providing a platform for progressive Pan-African perspectives on politics, development and global affairs. With more than 2,500 contributors across the continent and a readership of more than 660,000, Pambazuka News has become the indispensable source of authentic voices of Africa's social analysts and activists.

Pambazuka Press and Pambazuka News are published by Fahamu (www.fahamu.org)

Feminist Alternatives

 Feminist Alternatives (FemAL) is a group of feminist activists in South Africa working against sexism and oppression. They are committed to helping unite the voices and actions of women in poor and working-class communities across national boundaries and borders.

CONTENTS

ACKNOWLEDGEMENTS

A process which produces a body of work of this nature requires many hearts, many minds and much sweat. Nineteen feminist activists organised to come together over two days and reflect on women's human condition and within that women's organising in the context of a patriarchal, neoliberal social and world order.

We wear many hats, transcend borders and nationalities and share a dream. We speak here about our own lives, our grapplings with feminist organising as activists in our own right, not as representatives or spokespersons of organisations or social movements. We claim the contributions we make to the organisational sites of struggle in which we are located, but we speak as activists who transcend narrow definitions of organisations and sites of struggle.

We are Dora Barry (living and organising from Cape Town, originally from Ogoniland in the Niger Delta of Nigeria), Mary Yuin Tal (living and organising from Cape Town, originally from Ibalichum, Cameroon), Desiree Nolubabalo Higa (Khayelitsha), Mamy Tladi (Sebokeng Zone 3), Nosipho Twala (the Vaal), Zanele Gladys Mokolo (Orange Farm), Virginia Setshedi (Gauteng), Ntombolundi Zitha (Keiskammahoek, Eastern Cape), Zandile Nsibande (Kennedy Road, Durban), Promise Mthembu (KwaZulu Natal), Jean Beukes (Mitchell's Plain), Lorraine Heunis (Zille-Raine Heights), Davine Witbooi (Luitzville, Northern Cape), Ronald Wesso (living in Cape Town, organising in the Western Province and Northern Cape), Wendy Pekeur (living in Stellenbosch and organising in the Western Province and beyond), Shereen Essof (living and organising from Cape Town, originally from Zimbabwe), Koni Benson (Cape Town), Anna Davies-van Es (Cape Town), Sipho Mthathi (organising from Cape Town and Johannesburg).

\

By the time the 19 authors came together to crystalise our reflections, many people had given material fuel to the fire which kept the project going. Deborah Byrne, Rukia Cornelius, Ingrid Mentjies, Shereen Essof and Sipho Mthathi had co-founded the Feminist Collective, which later morphed into Feminist Alternatives (FemAL). FemAL conceptualised the project, convened the group and benefited greatly from the contributions of a publication reference group, consisting of Ronald Wesso, Koni Benson, Ingrid Meintjies, Shereen Essof and Sipho Mthathi, who gave over and above their "mandate" to see it through. Rukia Cornelius gave backup support and conceptual advice , inspiring ideas and asking hard questions to ensure that FemAL was accountable to its values in the way it undertook the project. Shamillah Wilson and Nosipho Twala also contributed as members of the FemAL Collective. Sipho Mthathi and subsequently Shereen Essof co-ordinated the project.

Yasmin Sooka lent the Foundation for Human Right's (FHR) infrastructure, time and staff, which together enabled the Collective to begin organising to the extent that it has thus far. We are grateful to Yasmin, Valerie Sebastian, Blessing Rufetu, Misty McWilliams, Millicent Pholosi and all at FHR who have provided financial accounting, systems, encouragement, logistical and other kinds of support to the Collective's work in 2008–2009.

We thank Oxfam and EED/CDT for the funding support which made the publication process possible. Specifically, Ayanda Mvimbi (then at Oxfam) and Gavin Andersson, who facilitated the funding and whose belief in our vision inspired us to dream. The Joint Gender Fund (JGF) also gave funding support for finalisation and printing of the publication and supports FemAL's ongoing activities.

Warda Essa (of WE Designs) turned words and images into art with her beautiful layout of this publication. Noel Franzen put his talent to bear and brought us the cover art, Vaun Cornell gave editorial services and much useful comment. Isaac Sikhakhane, Shamilla Wilson, Koni Benson, Shereen Essof, Rukia Cornellius and Pieter Levecque contributed photographic material that has been included in this publication. For which much thanks. Pambazuka Press partnered with FemAL in copublishing this book. To the Pambazuka team who rose up to the challenge of the project: Viva! Gabriella Van Heerden facilitated the art session during which women present at the workshop produced the art you see woven in the pages of this book.

We thank also, all the many friends, partners and social networks that gave encouragement, babysat, cooked, listened, subsidised and provided all manner of support to this project.

As FemAL, we have drawn inspiration from many feminist activists in South Africa and all around the world in the design of the methodology and process of this project and in many ways our larger vision. Sheroes, we thank you all for your courage and example. To those organising for and with Feminist Alternatives, we look forward to your own way of extending the conversations we have captured in this book.

Women farmworker rally, Stellenbosch, 2006.

Introduction
MY DREAM IS TO BE BOLD:
OUR WORK TO END PATRIARCHY

On 4th April 1981, hundreds of people from all over the Western Cape gathered in the hall of the St Francis Cultural Centre in Langa. People came from Paarl, Worcester, Wolsley, Stellenbosch, Montagu, Ashton, Elsies River. They came in minibuses, cars and by public transport. They were joined by women from Nyanga, Gugulethu and other parts of the Cape Flats to participate in the first Conference of the United Women's Organisation (UWO). At that meeting Dora Tamana spoke with fire in her heart:

"You who have no work, speak.

You who have no homes, speak.

You who have no schools, speak.

You who have to run like chickens from the vultures, speak.

We must share the problems so that we can solve them together.

We must free ourselves.

Men and women must share housework.

Men and women must work together in the home and out in the world.

There are no crèches and nursery schools for our children, no homes for the aged, or people to care for the sick.

Women must unite to fight for these rights.

We must go forward!

You who have no work, speak. You who have no homes, speak. You who have no schools, speak. You who have to run like chickens from the vultures, speak. We must share the problems so that we can solve them together. We must free ourselves.

The government put us in stables for horses, not houses.

There are no ceilings, no floors, no doors, but the rents are high.

We have to find a strong organisation to fight for us.

Now that we are gathered here, we can be strong, call the women to join.

Hambani Makhosikazi!

Mothers, release yourselves.

All the people who are crying for relief, people of all colours, come.

Senzenina? What have we done?

Women, stand together, build the organisation, make it strong."

Twenty-eight years later on 12th June 2009, 23 feminist activists from all around the country gathered at the Fountains Court in Cape Town. They came by plane, in cars, on scooters and by public transport. Women from Sebokeng, the Vaal, Orange Farm, Mitchell's Plain, Zille Raine Heights, Kuils River, Lutzville in the Northern Cape, Keiskammahoek in the Eastern Cape, Kennedy Road in Durban.

Had anything changed for the women in the room since Dora Tamana uttered those words in 1981? The women present knew intimately how the last 15 years in South Africa's history were stamped with two outstanding achievements: the birth of a constitutional state and multiparty democracy; and the constitutional commitment to eliminating discrimination, particularly racial and gendered discrimination. But the women present also knew about the betrayals that made these achievements empty.

For everyone, the post-1994 period was one of hope and promise. Women's struggles and organising efforts within and outside of the structures of the anti-

apartheid liberation movement mean that today women participate in key positions of power. In parliament and government as voters, legislators, members of the judiciary. In politics as members and leaders of political parties. In the socio-economic sector as civil society activists, political analysts, media agents, public servants, public intellectuals and more generally as citizens exercising their agency in the broad spectrum of their daily lives and that of the broader society. What women have won has been through their own organising efforts and thus the material conditions of many women living in South Africa have significantly improved with some becoming part of the wealthy elite.

But capitalist patriarchy is still intact. Its most recent manifestation, neoliberalism, leaves growing inequality and violence in its wake. The reality for many women is that gross inequalities continue to divide and haunt us. While the statistics sometimes don't look so bad they blur the reality of a society where the gap between the rich and poor is at its most stark and where women are affected the most.

NO WORK, NO HOMES

While all South Africans should have access to sanitation, the bucket system still exists leading to many health problems for the poor; there were a million farm evictions in the first ten years of the country's democracy, leading to an explosion of shack settlements; unemployment figures are at an all time high; as a young woman you can't attend school if you are pregnant and teenage pregnancy is on the rise; one in three women starts their sex life by force.

The majority of South Africa's poor are black working-class women. Of these, rural women, whose incomes are mainly from pensions and remittances from relatives, form the poorest of the poor which comprise 20% of households with an income of between R400 and R700 per month. Thirty-five percent of economically active women are unemployed. Forty-nine percent of employed black women work in occupations such as garbage collection, domestic work and farm work.

There is glaring inequality in access to productive and social resources like land, housing, electricity, water, healthcare, credit, information and education. Neoliberalism has impacted particularly negatively in this regard with the privatisation of social services. For every household that does not have access to running water or electricity, a woman's time and labour are compromised. In non-urban areas, three in every ten households (30%) have to fetch wood for cooking and heating purposes. Households with piped water inside the dwelling increased from 60.4% in 1996 to 62.3% in 2007. Households that used electricity for cooking increased from 47.1% in 1996 to 51.4% in 2007. The percentage of households with World Health Organisation (WHO) standards of sanitation increased from 50.3% in 1996 to 53.8% in 2007. What exactly do these statistics mean?

Women's land and housing rights are still limited and insecure. Too many women continue to live in poverty, struggling from the multiple impacts of HIV/AIDS and a failing healthcare system that deprioritises women's sexual and reproductive health needs. The major causes of female deaths in South Africa are: high blood pressure; pregnancy-related complications; prolonged labour and obstetric haemorrhage; septic abortions; HIV/AIDS related diseases; cancer of the cervix; tuberculosis; malaria; and other opportunistic diseases. Violence has become a part of the daily lives of women, with most of it happening with impunity. Sexism and male domination are reflected in the rapes, femicides, forms of gender based and sexual violence and misogyny that have today reached crisis proportions. One in every three women in South Africa is in an abusive relationship. A woman is killed by her partner every six days and there is a rape every 35 seconds. This is a national disaster requiring emergency measures.[2]

For women, freedom has not yet translated into reality. Precisely how male domination and female subordination in society works and the ways in which it affects the quality of our lives differ sharply according to race, class and sexual orientation. But ultimately what unites us as women across the diversity of our race, class, sexual orientation, religion, socio-economic and citizenship status is that we live in a misogynist society. After decades and decades of organising for women's liberation, why is this so?

CHICKENS AND VULTURES

In South Africa today, we are facing the failure of and reaction to an attempt to end patriarchy via paper. Commitments to ending gender inequality through enshrining clauses in constitutions, via parliamentary legislation, state policy and national gender machineries, are not unique to South Africa. But policy reform is not an end in itself. It cannot be allowed to replace or subordinate the goal of dismantling patriarchy for that of consolidating political power and capital.

An important detour is necessary here. Many people are uncomfortable with the word feminism. It is often understood as anti-nationalist and pro-imperialist. This is partly because it's been turned into a "dirty" word by those who don't like to see women stepping out of line, claiming equality, behaving autonomously,

> *For women, freedom has not yet translated into reality. Precisely how male domination and female subordination in society works and the ways in which it affects the quality of our lives differ sharply according to race, class and sexual orientation.*

> **The feminism we need is, for a start, grounded in our context.**
> **It is anti-essentialist.**
> **It sees gender as lived in many different ways.**
> **So it makes sense to talk about masculinities and femininities in the plural. It sees identities, including masculine and feminine identities, as being fluid and changeable, varying from one time and place to another."**

creating a new politics. For this reason women's liberation movements have a lot of enemies. But feminism is indispensable as a programme.

In reclaiming feminism we need to specify which variety because there's not one feminism, there are many, just as there are many versions of socialism. It is open to us, in each new political conjuncture, to distinguish between the different versions and choose the theory and the political practice that's relevant to inform our change agendas and struggles. We need concepts, thinking tools, that reflect our reality and serve our purpose.

The feminism we need is, for a start, grounded in our context. It is anti-essentialist. It sees gender as lived in many different ways. So it makes sense to talk about masculinities and femininities in the plural. It sees identities, including masculine and feminine identities, as being fluid and changeable, varying from one time and place to another. It's not an individualist but a collective feminism, measuring success not by how high a woman can climb, but by the condition in which most women remain. This is at the heart of the South African problem. The few who have risen up the socio-economic and political ladder are held up as examples, which is important. But too often the few mask the majority who continue to live in poverty and struggle to survive.

The feminism we need goes beyond simply remarking on the difference between women's and men's life experiences, whereby men are everything that women are not, and vice versa. No. It must see in that process of differentiation that power and inequality are involved. Men in our societies have the power to define women as "other" and in so doing to define them as of lesser value. Feminism sees this "othering" process as having brought into being a structure of gender power.

A feminism of this kind sees, tries to understand and above all to challenge this patriarchal gender order. That's what it's for. But we want to take one step more now, and carry this feminism out beyond the struggle with patriarchy, into an engagement with other oppressive systems, such as, in the current South African context, nationalism and militarism, which are both ideologies (mindsets) and practices that flow from patriarchy.

Nationalism refers to an ideology, sentiment or a form of culture that focuses on the nation. Its goal is to establish, take over, empower and enrich a particular nation state at the expense of oppressing non-members. It usually has a distinct vision of ethnic identity and political behaviour that is proper for members of the nation. This is often rooted in patriarchy. Militarism claims that the military is the foundation of society's security. Sexist behaviour and values associated with the military are promoted and celebrated.

These "brother" ideologies have very similar consequences for women and men, for gender relations. Patriarchy, nationalism and militarism are a kind of mutual admiration society. Nationalism is in love with patriarchy because patriarchy offers it women who'll breed true little patriots. Militarism is in love with patriarchy because its women offer up their sons to be soldiers. Patriarchy is in love with nationalism and militarism because they produce unambiguously masculine men and submissive women or women who behave like men.

In South Africa today new forms of patriarchy masked as a conservative traditionalism and militarism are on the increase. Some examples can be found in the uptake by popular culture of things like the song "*Umshini Wami / we baba / awuleth' Umshini Wami*" (my machine gun / oh father / please bring me my machine

> *In South Africa today new forms of patriarchy masked as a conservative traditionalism and militarism are on the increase.*

gun), a song historically associated with the liberation struggle but now adopted in an unreconstructed way as the signature tune of President Jacob Zuma. It is not only militaristic but carries *heteronormative* sexual innuendo, and it entangles us in a seamless masculinity with little place for a range of gendered identities in the current dispensation. The same is true of embracing the "100% Zulu Boy" discourse. The other aspect of this puzzle is neoliberalism.

Neoliberal capitalist agendas have intersected with patriarchy, nationalism and militarism in ways that have reasserted and redefined the roles of men and women, as well as who constitutes a citizen in this country. The hate crimes that we are witnessing – xenophobic attacks against "immigrants", the rape of lesbians, the stripping of women who are wearing mini skirts – are all examples of the violence of transgression of this triage and the identities that it constructs and condones. We have to ask: what does this mean for women and society at large?

In this period too, our political language of struggle as women has been usurped, hijacked by the system and depoliticised. Thabo Mbeki, more than any other president male or female, took the project of liberal feminism further than anyone else. What do we mean by this? Let us think about liberal feminism as a focus on women's liberation within the system of a liberal capitalist democracy. This is what the Mbeki Project was all about. For this reason then there was a drive to give women equal representation. But this was done within the existing system (bourgeois authoritarianism) and power structures of the state without necessarily changing them. Another example of this was about enacting laws that guarantee women a limited number of rights. These rights are protected, to a limited extent, from a range of possible violations that occur everyday. It gave women recourse to the law, to equal representation as it is invoked by the language of quotas and gender parity. Ultimately, it opens up the project of building South Africa as a competitive capitalist democracy to the participation of women.

Now, obviously there have been various problems with this approach. The important question to consider here is: are they problems of insufficient commitment and implementation of the project of gender equality? Or are they problems that stem from the limitations of the project itself? This was a project that was never about abolishing capitalist patriarchy, but rather about addressing gender inequality in ways that are not threatening and that maintain the status quo.

And in 2009, we have the laboratory result of what you get if you fight patriarchy within those limitations. Our context is supposedly different to that of Dora Tamana. Whilst today we may be considered citizens, the majority still have no homes, no schools and have to run like chickens from the vultures. We have a lovely language of democracy but the lives of the majority have become harder. While women are still finding a voice, developing a language to explain the reality and defining a feminism, women are organising for life.

WOMEN, STAND TOGETHER. BUILD THE ORGANISATION. MAKE IT STRONG

The depth of sexism in South African society has to be unmasked. If you look at what women have actually gained in the last ten years in terms of gender equality and participation in broader socio-economic and political spheres, it's a lot, but not enough. We need way more than this. Yet society's reaction to the limited gains that women have made elicits such a violent backlash from the defenders

> "*Yet society's reaction to the limited gains that women have made elicits such a violent backlash from the defenders of sexism and patriarchy. This is proof of the depth of sexism that we are currently witnessing. Apart from the issue of violence, which is ever present at the level of the tone of the debate and spirit of the times, many gains that women have made are being eroded.*"

of sexism and patriarchy. This is proof of the depth of sexism that we are currently witnessing. Apart from the issue of violence, which is ever present at the level of the tone of the debate and spirit of the times, many gains that women have made are being eroded.

For a woman activist taking on the struggle of freedom for women, there are many platforms from which to fight. In South Africa there is a long history of feminist activists located within movements whose primary interest is not feminist, like working class movements, unions and community organisations. A lot of time has been spent thinking about how to make these formations more feminist, how to "mainstream" a women's agenda.

But these attempts have contributed to deflating and diluting the feminist spirit and agenda because the "starting point" must always be negotiated or fought for. Neoliberalism has contributed to masking the distribution of power, which is still in favour of men. In this kind of context there is always need to justify the focus on the liberation of women as a means to some other end, whether it's national liberation, socialism or working class emancipation, and despite the fight against sexism being politically correct and sometimes strategic for leftist organisations to have women on board. In this kind of context women are disadvantaged from the start, often losing more than is won and leaving us feeling alone, disillusioned and weighed down by having to be vigilant and fight, at every turn, to right the wrongs being done to us by the organisational forms we choose to work within as well as by the system within which we live.

Is this adequate? In an environment of deepening polarisation, alienation and misogyny when the world's socio-economic and political paradigms are failing us,

> *" Women do the hard work in supporting and building the struggles and organisations but the campaigns are designed in ways that are neither woman-friendly nor accommodating of women's agendas. "*

it is important as feminist activists that we re-evaluate our strategy in order to be clear about which platforms allow us to engage in activism that contributes to building a free world for women and all people by dismantling and overthrowing patriarchy and its allied systems in an unfettered way.

If we look at the people who are most affected by any issue facing us in South Africa and the region, if we look at the people who are out there organising in order to survive, the majority are poor and working-class women most of whom are black. Women attend community meetings in large numbers. They take to the streets in protest. Due to our socialisation and reproductive roles, it is women who are constantly thinking about where the next meal, the next pre-paid water voucher, or instalment of school fees is going to come from. Things become even more interesting if we go a little further. If you look at the leadership of many of these struggles for basic services it is often predominantly male and you never hear this layer of leadership asking: "Where are the women in this agenda? When are the women going to speak?"

It's the same old patriarchal story: women do the hard work in supporting and building the struggles and organisations but the campaigns are designed in ways that are neither woman-friendly nor accommodating of women's agendas. When women challenge male leadership in our moments of radicalism around our own agendas we find that the spaces become hostile and our male comrades and friends turn on us in order to whip us into line, a male line, and other women become agents that police our radicalism too.

This raises critical questions for women's organising and how we engage in mixed gender spaces and struggles. How do we organise as women drawing on

> *This raises critical questions for women's organising and how we engage in mixed gender spaces and struggles. How do we organise as women drawing on our own sense of power and agency? Currently, not only are our needs not being addressed, spaces and opportunities to further radical struggle are being lost.*
> *Are we satisfied with doing the same things in the same way?*

> *It's very hard for an individual feminist activist to find a home. That home has to be created because the reality is that everyone agrees with women's liberation but they think it's compatible with women's oppression and that is a very difficult situation to be in. It is a big liberation then, for women to create their own autonomous spaces that are unapologetic for their orientation.*

our own sense of power and agency? Currently, not only are our needs not being addressed, spaces and opportunities to further radical struggle are being lost. Are we satisfied with doing the same things in the same way? Are our actions taking us closer to where we want to be, if our ultimate goal is the emancipation of all women? We've come a long way and that has to be acknowledged and celebrated. But we have not arrived.

It's very hard for an individual feminist activist to find a home. That home has to be created because the reality is that everyone agrees with women's liberation but they think it's compatible with women's oppression and that is a very difficult situation to be in. It is a big liberation then, for women to create their own autonomous spaces that are unapologetic for their orientation.

FEMINIST ALTERNATIVES

It is this understanding that led to the decision by a number of women from South and Southern Africa to begin asking the questions: how do we organise from a clear feminist perspective and create spaces that allow women to claim the title of being a feminist? How do we begin to disturb the established understandings and ways of conducting struggle? How can we organise to overthrow patriarchy? After much discussion, debate, consultation and action, based on our reading of the socio-economic and political context as well as our analysis of women's organising nationally, regionally and globally, Feminist Alternatives (FemAL) was born.

FemAL is a group of feminist activists desperate for meaningful alternatives to leadership, power and real social transformation where women, and all people, can be free to realise their full potential and humanity.[3] Geographically located

March against prepaid water meters and new devices to limit water to those with money, Mitchell's Plain, 2007.

in South Africa, the FemAL collective has worked and organised nationally and globally against sexism and oppression. Through FemAL, we have committed to build an initiative that helps unite the voices and actions of women in poor and working-class communities across national boundaries and borders for a more cohesive, effective impact.

As part of FemAL's work we were interested in finding ways of creating knowledge and sparking or catalysing action that actively contributed to challenging the power imbalances embedded in knowledge production. We felt that this process had to start from the diverse range of experiences of radical feminist activists. We were committed to refusing the fragmentation of knowledge and avoiding dichotomous and other forms of patriarchal thinking, building on the wisdom of individual women in respectful dialogue and on the complex and multi-layered thinking required for successful feminist organising in moving forward, and ultimately engaging in a collaborative publishing process. We were also aware that because of women's socialisation and position within society, writing often frightens us and we rarely have the luxury of time and space to write. It is hard to do. But it is a fundamental part of our activism and claiming our voice.

What you have in your hands today is the fruition of this process: a process that brought together, in its totality, 25 feminist activists from around the country in order to engage in a reflective sharing, writing and publication process – an ambitious task, but one that was met with generosity, excitement, enthusiasm and creativity.

> " *FemAL is a group of feminist activists desperate for meaningful alternatives to leadership, power and real social transformation where women, and all people, can be free to realise their full potential and humanity.* "

THE EXPERIMENT

The FemAL publication reference group that undertook this project was aware that we could write a book from a feminist perspective about the most radical women on the frontline of struggle by travelling around the country, interviewing each woman and, in typical research fashion, editing, analysing and presenting conclusions.[4] We chose not to do that.

Instead we embarked on an experiment. We wanted to create a space where women could come together in an unburdened way in order to embark on a process in which we could hear not just individual stories but have women activists in conversation with each other reflecting on our collective work: is it getting us to where we really need to get to, can we learn from each other in terms of experiences, energy and strategies? Is this taking us closer to our goal of overthrowing patriarchy and if not, then what? We wanted to be able to really get to the core of our organising in ways that we often cannot do in other spaces for fear of discomfort or over-exposure. We wanted the process to be liberating as the final product. We wanted to build collective analysis through speaking to other women, comparing experience, collectively trying to understand that experience and theorise it.

As part of this process we met via both virtual and physical spaces.[5] The main publication workshop was held on 12th and 13th June 2009 in Cape Town. Clusters of tables allowed for group work and a circle of chairs to one side of the room allowed for intimate plenary discussions. Background music or the voices of women singing were never far away, flowers and fruit, sweets, tea and coffee readily available. Women were given notebooks and pens to record their personal

> *As part of FemAL's work we were interested in finding ways of creating knowledge and sparking or catalysing action that actively contributed to challenging the power imbalances embedded in knowledge production.*

" *The FemAL publication reference group that undertook this project was aware that we could write a book from a feminist perspective about the most radical women on the frontline of struggle by travelling around the country, interviewing each woman and in typical research fashion, editing, analysing and presenting conclusions. We chose not to do that.* "

reflections and funky socks to keep toes warm as we worked way into the night. Women brought posters and banners that very quickly adorned the walls and made the meeting room ours.

The process unfolded through an initial plenary that set the context, collectively established the collective basis for the work and laid the foundation with regards to the idea of collective publishing, ethics and process. After intense discussion and debate on this as well as issues of political orientation and the underpinnings of FemAL's work, we moved very quickly in a way that allowed the people present to share deeply. Women divided up into groups of two or three plus a scribe.[6] Participants were given an interview guide with basic interview tips as well as guiding questions. The ensuing conversations/interviews were facilitated and conducted by the women present within the groups whilst the scribe recorded on computer in a pre-designed template, the word-for-word transcript of the interview.[7] Whilst participants took an extended break, scribes tidied up the transcripts in terms of spelling and grammar and the now "cleaned" up interviews were handed back to the groups together with an editing guide so that further editing could take place in order to ensure that each woman present was comfortable and happy with her story.[8] This was done overnight.

ART AS A MEANS FOR SOCIAL CHANGE

In the evening of the first day a facilitated art session was conducted by Gabriella Van Heerden.[9] Art that is defined as a collective cultural production has the potential to support women's rebellion and resistance and can be a tool to allow for alternative social relations that challenge capitalism's constant pressure

to commodify ourselves and our relations to others. Art can act as a space of encounter, where the meaning(s) of the piece(s) are constantly being re-produced by the audience, regenerating and revealing histories/herstories, sharing struggles, and proposing questions to think differently about how we relate to ourselves and our community.

In a relaxed setting, amidst lots of art supplies, we were led into a guided visualisation/meditation about our contexts. Following on from this we were invited to draw our world, the site from which we come. After the visual representation of our location, we had to name and overlay in the art piece the words that encapsulated or indicated an overthrowing of patriarchy.

Most of the artwork in this publication was produced in this session over much song, wine and laughter. The individual pieces produced stand alone, but together also form a mural of communal celebrations of resistance and rebellion through the subject matter presented. The art pieces contribute to our production of knowledge and analysis of our current situation, and challenge us to regenerate anti-capitalist, anti-racist, anti-homophobic, and anti-sexist social relations. Art as a tool that can be a medium to spread or disseminate analysis, and re-member the process of dreaming and hope for a different world, a world where many worlds fit. The re-dreaming is also a challenge to ourselves to ask the difficult questions of what next.

The second day began with a gallery walk, taking in the art produced overnight. Much of the second day was devoted to plenary discussion that fed into a collective analysis of the individual stories and began drawing on the art gallery as a powerful representation of our lives and struggles as women. This set

" Art that is defined as a collective cultural production has the potential to support women's rebellion and resistance and can be a tool to allow for alternative social relations that challenge capitalism's constant pressure to commodify ourselves and our relations to others. "

" Women owned and shaped the space and process and we were all respectful of the feminist principles: the personal is political; the centring of women's experience; creating of alternatives; trust; honouring what it was that women shared and agreeing that nothing would be published without full consent. "

of plenary conversations broadened out and began to further contextualise and grapple with an explanation or theory for why we are where we are as women at this historical conjuncture.

Participants at the workshop requested that the experiences of reference group members who were facilitating should also be included in the publication and this was done outside of the workshop space but using the same methodology. There were some women who were not able to attend the workshop for various logistical reasons and plans were made to interview them separately and together so that the spirit of the process could be maintained. Women express themselves in different ways and women were encouraged to make available supporting materials like poems, photographs or anything that they thought would further strengthen and texture their story as well as the entire publication.

The reference group met numerous times post-workshop – in re-looking at the material and pulling together all the moving parts of the publication. Updates and follow-ups with women were undertaken in the process of finalising transcripts as well as collating supporting materials. The process was not perfect. We tried to hold the space open and not rush people forward by shutting people out or up. Writing can often be an intense and time-consuming process and we found that we needed to assign responsibility to teams of people for the development of this introduction as well as the last two chapters of the book: "Already bold we must be even bolder", and "Out of the pages of this volume". In this process we tried to be as consultative and inclusive as possible. Women owned and shaped the space and process and we were all respectful of the feminist principles: the personal is political; the centring of women's experience; creating of alternatives;

trust; honouring what it was that women shared and agreeing that nothing would be published without full consent. Warda spent countless hours doing the design and layout and, whilst staying true to the vision of the project, Vaun Cornell worked with us as copy editor in an effort to "make dreams come true".

A radical feminist movement builds on the actions and words contained on the pages that follow. Such a movement has to make continual, daily choices about its positioning and practice. We have to reflect deeply, develop our strategy and tactics smartly, choose our discourse intelligently and give thought to the slogans we paint on our placards, the words we type in our leaflets, the press releases we issue in our campaigns. As the pages of this book testify, we believe we can't get these choices right, in ever-shifting political situations, without a radical feminist analysis to guide us.

Endnotes

1. Developed and written by Shereen Essof and Ronald Wesso in consultation with contributing authors.
2. Statistics SA General Household Survey 2007 and South African Police Crime Statistics 2005.
3. Feminist Alternatives is run by a collective currently comprised of Rukia Cornelius, Shereen Essof, Sipho Mthathi, Nosipho Twala and Shamillah Wilson. As Feminist Alternatives moves forward with its work the collective will be expanded accordingly.
4. Koni Benson, Shereen Essof, Ingrid Menjities, Sipho Mthathi and Ronald Wesso.
5. Including via e-mail, telephone and fax.
6. Koni Benson, Anna Davies-van Es, Shereen Essof, Jessica Thorn, Sipho Mthathi and Thobela Joni.
7. See appendix 1.
8. See appendix 2.
9. From Circle Stories, based at the Frank Joubert Art Centre, Cape Town, South Africa.

Nosipho Twala

My name is Nosipho Twala. It means "gift". Sipho means "big gift" – me, I am just one gift.

I think I wear many caps, but I will speak about Remmoho[1] here. Remmoho is a women's forum. It is a space that was created for women in the Anti-Privatisation Forum (APF). We decided to form this space because of the organisational culture of the APF.

The APF is a social movement, so they understand social justice and articulate positions on gender equality. But when you look at the position of women and how women are treated, you see that it is not a women-friendly organisation.

Remmoho was formed to be a source for change in all social movements. Women must be able to speak, women must feel free and they must feel part of the organisation. Because if you look at the composition of organisations, the majority are women, but the leadership is men.

It is the same thing Dora Barry described – women felt inadequate and not accepted, they felt that they didn't have the political language and they didn't see this as their space. They are informed by patriarchy and believe that men are the ones who can articulate and speak and say things in the "correct" language. We wanted to build women's activism and we're slowly working on women's leadership.

> **We know that putting women in positions of power without proper support can expose them to backlash, all forms of violence and emotional abuse.**

Through Remmoho we have put a woman in leadership at APF. Mamy is now the Chairperson. But we know that putting women in positions of power without proper support can expose them to backlash, all forms of violence and emotional abuse. This means that as an organisation we will have to focus all our energy on trying to deal with the backlash.

We also need to start working on women's confidence and have them recognise what they do as powerful. We have to change women's mindsets, women who think that you have to know what *Das Kapital* is, or who Marx is, or that they need to know "big English" or even good English.

As Remmoho we focus on language as a tool. Because English was used to oppress and eliminate women from discussion, we encourage women to break through this and to speak English. But we also take time to explain difficult concepts, where we can ask questions and speak in our own language. This means that women will not be marginalised because they don't understand the language of the oppressor or when some of the things get lost in translation. Most women are not given an opportunity to attend workshops because there is no translation and they don't understand English. For instance, most women were excluded from the World Social Forum (2008) and the AWID Forum (which took place in Cape Town in November 2008) based on their level of understanding English.

VISION FOR WOMEN

At the heart of this work is that we realise a lot of women are doing things on their own initiative. We must help women to realise this and recognise their organising work as important.

We want to be emancipated, to be empowered, to create as many spaces for women as possible, because when you look at women in these spaces they are different people: the richness, the respect, and the experience that women bring. We want to be embraced, to see women as leaders, leading these struggles and being able to have a voice.

Voice is the door to many things – to improved access, to raised consciousness, to challenge both formal and informal laws. This is important, because if we only work in one block, like only raising consciousness, but don't challenge informal cultural rules, we will not be able to see the shifts.

> "*We have to change women's mindsets, women who think that you have to know what* **Das Kapital** *is, or who Marx is, or that they need to know "big English" or even good English.*"

" Voice is the door to many things – to improved access, to raised consciousness, to challenge both formal and informal laws. This is important, because if we only work in one block, like only raising consciousness, but don't challenge informal cultural rules, we will not be able to see the shifts. "

CONTEXT

The socio-economic impact is complex and threatening to women's lives, physically and otherwise. Firstly, most women are unemployed, and even if they are employed, they are employed as casuals, or as temps. This hampers women's ability to organise. If people have to work on Saturdays, there is no standard day when we can get everyone together. Temporary work also compromises women's rights as workers. The fact is that even when women work, they still have to come home and cook and clean. Women have no time, and this really affects organising.

The fact that most organisations do not have a childcare policy is also a problem. In our organisation, we have to debate how old a child must be to provide childcare. Because if I have a 12-year-old the organisation thinks the child is old enough to stay home. This discourages women from participating. So we have to apply feminist thinking to everything. In South Africa, is it safe to leave a 12-year-old at home alone? But due to budget constraints and shrinking funding, we need to make detrimental decisions that sometimes hamper our organising. Because sometimes we have to say that if a woman has five children, we will only pay for two, forcing her to leave the others at home. This discourages and hampers activism.

When we work as Remmoho, we work with women's organisations. They speak about all the "big things" they are doing, but when you get to know them, you find out about all the other vital things they are doing, yet these things are not seen as important. This is linked to funding – most women's projects can't access funding because they don't have the language to articulate what they are doing in a way that shows the value of their work to those who make the financial decisions. Funders will say "no, this is just a small group of women taking care of the aged",

"We have to change women's mindsets, women who think that you have to know what Das Kapital is, or who Marx is, or that they need to know 'Big English' or even good English."

> " *If you ask women to write their bios you will get two sentences, but if you sit down and interview them, talk to them, you will get a book. It has to do with the way we are raised and this is gendered. Men can do it so easily. Women always play down their contribution.* "

but if you meet them, you see that they are doing advocacy work, challenging formal laws, challenging the system. But they don't have language to say what they are doing. But if a man comes into the organisation – in three weeks he can tell the world what he is doing, and he is not even doing it!

The fact that we don't see what we are doing as important work is gendered. This also means that we don't see it as our successes. In all the processes I have been involved in, if you ask women to write their bios you will get two sentences, but if you sit down and interview them, talk to them, you will get a book. It has to do with the way we are raised and this is gendered. Men can do it so easily. Women always play down their contribution.

South Africa's new government, with Jacob Zuma as leader, has given rise to so many challenges, and I think as women we need to unite. The media glorifies and portrays polygamy as a good thing. The attitude of men in the street has changed regarding rape and HIV. And now everything is cultural, ethnic, Zulu and rooted. I think as the women's movement we focused too much on Zuma, on criticising him. It really made him a hero and that was not the angle to go. It made him a big big hero, and most men view this as a very good shift and that we need to go back to our roots. I don't think culture is all bad, but some of the thinking is dangerous for women, especially what Zuma has said in the media about women and young girls. This means that we have to strengthen our work.

The more people criticised Zuma – take the Zille[2] criticism – the more people supported him. It polarised the debate between ethnicity, and people identified with Zuma because he is black. Zille was seen as a racist white bitch. It became a battle of race and class rather than a gender debate.

Remmoho did work around these issues, but people went to the polls and voted for Zuma in big numbers, standing in long queues to ensure that he won. Women stood and voted – most people supporting him are women. We made him a hero.

VICTORIES

I don't quantify victories in big numbers, but to see two or three women articulate their issues who weren't able to speak before, is a highlight. I am also happy to see women value these spaces, and how these spaces lead us to shift our practices at home – how we raise children, how we relate to our partners, what issues to challenge in our communities and how we are not being complacent about our achievements but pushing to ensure that we continue with this work.

We managed even to get semi-autonomy from the APF as women. We were able to organise marches against violence against women. We've had recognition from different places, even from across the globe, for the work we are doing. And we were able to work as a collective and bypass all the myths that women fight when they get together. And we have built our capacity.

CHALLENGES

We've had a major disappointment that we felt took us back ten steps. It involved a rape case, within the APF. The way it was handled by the organisation was disappointing – instead of the APF taking a stand, they said Remmoho must take a stand. The most difficult part has been the dynamics in handling this situation. We wanted to do more for the woman (the complainant), but the court stopped any contact because we are associated with the APF.

> *I don't quantify victories in big numbers, but to see two or three women articulate their issues who weren't able to speak before, is a highlight.*

Our private space is political. Most women have two voices: one for the public and one for the private space. They can be strong and articulate in public, but the practice is different. This is the reality that most women are living because of fear of violence and backlash. This shows me how complex the situation is. I also think this is a weakness of the organisation; I don't feel it is ready to deal with violence and backlash.

MOVING FORWARD

To confront with respect. To realise that the private is political, we need to begin to see the shifts in the private spaces because it is of no value if we are powerful in public spaces but can't change or interrogate informal and formal rules. To recognise the value of building women's activism, and that it will not be a once off process, but a process that we continually need to build on, by sharing and enriching our knowledge through others' experience.

To document these processes so we can have them as resources and recognise the work women are doing, but this hasn't been told through the eyes and through the voice of the women. To see what we are doing as important, is one of the steps that will bring change in our organisation, in our community and in our families.

I see ourselves as valuable citizens, and deserving of a life of quality. When you ask women what they want for themselves, their first answer is "I want a better place for my children". They can't say I want to have good sex, a car, or quality of life. They don't see themselves as deserving this.

Most importantly, we need to make sure that the work we do as feminists, as women, is valued. All this volunteering – it's gendered that women do incredible

> " *We need to begin to see the shifts in the private spaces because it is of no value if we are powerful in public spaces but can't change or interrogate informal and formal rules.* "

work but for free. We must recognise what we do as important and deserving of remuneration. We must see it as work.

I think at the centre of all this is sexuality. Women need to win that battle, which is part of us always seeing ourselves as owned by men. We are supposed to do things for men, but we still have hate crimes, like lesbian women being killed. Sexuality is central to all this. Once you realise that "I am the owner of my body" and that we don't have to apologise to our husbands, or our in-laws, that we can do what we want, we will begin to win the battle.

Endnotes

1. http://apf.org.za/article.php3?id_article=193.
2. Helen Zille is Premier of the Western Cape and leader of South Africa's official opposition party, the Democratic Alliance.

> "*Once you realise that "I am the owner of my body" and that we don't have to apologise to our husbands, or our in-laws, that we can do what we want, we will begin to win the battle.*"

WOMEN EMPOWE
POLE FOR NETWORK
HOTSUN
DROP OF RAIN
S.S. SCHOOL
GRAVEL ROAD
MUD HOUSE
DRY GRASS
VEGTABLE GARDEN
gate
PIT TOILET

Ntombolundi Zitha

I am from the Keiskammahoek in the Eastern Cape. It is a rural area. I live in Ward 11, Amahlathi Municipality. It is not easy to work in my area because our villages are scattered. You take long to get to our village. And we have no transport so we walk by foot whether it's hot or cold or raining. Our ward councillor is very useless. I am also a writer. I am not a very educated woman but I have a voice inside me.

STAND PIPE

I have raised four children as a single parent. I am not working. I survive by doing permaculture homestead gardening and I get a state grant. I look after my mother who gets an old age grant. I was helped a lot by the Border Rural Committee (BRC).[1] I was struggling. But I am a survivor. I know how to find ways to make sure my family has food every day. In 2000 I attended a workshop on women and writing. I write poems and short stories.

Each month the BRC gives me seeds. I have a water tank. It takes 300,000 litres. We have our own plot, our own water tank and our own bank account. A self-help project makes a difference for women because our children don't say "*Tata ndilambile*" – "Father, I am hungry" – anymore. We don't depend on social grants or food parcels as much. I'm proud of myself. I am proud because I provide for myself. I am proud because of my vegetable donations, especially to the old age people, or those who don't have something to eat, and those who are sick.

It does not solve all our problems, but it makes a difference for women, to be independent. We are 40 in this project, most of us are women.

We still struggle with land. Even though the land belongs to the government the chiefs say it's their land and they want to decide how it will be used. They don't like giving land to women. But we challenge this and slowly we begin to get land.

ORGANISING

I work a lot with the community, especially on issues of development. I was working at the Masivuke HIV/AIDS project as a volunteer caregiver. I learnt a lot from them. I understand sharing experiences with another person, how to solve problems, how to deal with issues and decision-making.

I help many people write residential letters when they need to apply for social grants. I also help other ones who have no money. I refer people to social workers to demand food parcels when there is nothing to eat. I talk to people who don't understand their illness and get them to go to the healthcare centre. Many people use herbalists' medicine even though they don't get better, because they don't know they could get help at the clinic. But, sometimes even if you go there is no medicine and they send you home.

We started Ikamvalethu Lamakhosikazi in May 2009 because we saw that there is no future for us women. Men dominate us. We need to think about our future. We need our own organisation that is not linked to political parties or civic groups, but one that can focus on the problems facing women.

Because there are long distances from one village to the next, we took a decision to form satellite groups in the villages to make things happen. Our local branch of Ikamva Lamakhosikazi is Iliso Lokhanyo, which means "the eye of light". Each village is represented by two members and the top five office bearers represent each village. The leadership cannot take any decision without consulting the local members. Our main aim is to have a sustainable community.

I know everyone says, "Why do you struggle in the rural areas? Things will never get better. You must go to the cities." But we are not convinced. We can't all pack up and go to the cities. The cities have become dangerous places. People lose their sense of community when they go there, and everyone is fighting for a little bit of the same thing. There is not enough for everyone.

I don't believe that a woman like me has a better chance in the cities. That is why we must think about our sustainability where we are. We have to at least keep

> *We still struggle with land. Even though the land belongs to the government the chiefs say it's their land and they want to decide how it will be used. They don't like giving land to women. But we challenge this and slowly we begin to get land.*

> *We started Ikamvalethu Lamakhosikazi in May 2009 because we saw that there is no future for us women. Men dominate us. We need to think about our future. We need our own organisation that is not linked to political parties or civic groups, but one that can focus on the problems facing women.*

trying. The challenge is how to make sure that we also get some of the things we need which can help make our lives easier: electricity, water, good sanitation, good houses, better schools for our children, how to produce our own food, and those things. We have to put our brains together. That is what we are trying to do.

I'm a founding member of Ntabakandoda Heritage Festival Formation. I am in the executive committee. Ntabakandoda was used by traditional leaders in the past. It is a holy place in the Amatola Mountains, where chief Maqoma wamaRharhabe was buried. People used to go there to worship and pray in times of trouble. Today, our vision is to use Ntabakandoda to create jobs. We want to turn it into a tourist and conference centre. Our aim is to get the community to understand the importance of our heritage, and to mobilise them to participate. It could help us reduce the high rate of unemployment among young people. Our children can't always go to the urban areas for opportunities. There aren't jobs there either. We have to find ways to get them to be part of the process of building our rural areas. It is hard but we must try. I am heartsore when I see young people go to the towns hoping to get jobs. Then many of them hang around *ematyotyombeni* and have no work. Maybe we can do something good with Ntabakandoda.

In the women's organisation we have young women. Sometimes young women don't want to be involved. Then they have problems when employment opportunities come. Women must be empowered. Women must not be afraid to talk about their problems. Skills are needed. Children pass matric but there are no opportunities for them to learn computer skills. Many parents here don't have money to send our children to colleges although we would like to; they are too expensive.

CHALLENGES

It is a challenge to build a feminist movement; to mobilise young women to be part of the organisation. Young people have many problems. They need communication skills to build their confidence to speak and be involved. They need experience in how to deal with people and social problems. We need to learn to do our own research. Some women do not talk because of their culture. We need to convince them about their rights.

Computer skills are needed because our community is isolated and we lack information on many things. It is hard for us to dream and see other options because of this. It is hard to be connected. From the grassroots level to the national, we must be connected, all of us. We can be strong if we are connected as women.

VISION

I went to school but couldn't finish because of money, and I had to look after my mother. I come from a poor home. I want to learn computer skills – I need to learn computer skills to make things easy. I'm not near to the town, I spend lots of money to print things and on transport. If the computers are here, things can be easier. I want to learn business skills, development planning, governance and community development. I want to learn community participation. I want to learn many things.

I've learnt through my community work that just because you are not very educated doesn't mean you must stop dreaming or building yourself up; you mustn't stop taking yourself seriously.

I am frustrated when as women we do all the hard things. *Amadoda ayekelela umxakatho*, they leave us with many burdens and sometimes they give up. We do so many things to keep the families and communities going. But we don't want that to be used to oppress us and undermine our contribution. When they say, "oh women are such good people, look at them, they help the poor and the sick", that is undermining. The government must do its side; we will do our side. We are tired of empty promises. We want to be taken seriously as full people and what we do for our homes and communities must be treated as important. There is so much I want.

Women in rural areas must speak out. We must not hide our problems. Women must be vocal. We are not powerless. Women must learn to share their ideas with each other. That is why we need spaces of our own to figure out things for ourselves, together.

I am happy if women initiate self-help income generation projects – to create jobs for the community so we can stop depending on men. For example, some women have their own equipment like sewing machines. We can make uniforms for the schools. The churches could also buy uniforms.

In rural areas we live in mud houses. We want decent houses. We are victims of disasters every year. We don't have roads. If it rains, cars don't come to our areas. It is like we are locked in. We can't go anywhere unless we have a horse.

We need electric lights. We live in darkness in our villages. It is not safe for women. Our girls are victimised in the dark.

I demand equal education. I will be happy if the government can close the gap between rural areas and urban areas in service delivery.

I want to see more women wake up and take up opportunities as feminist activists.

My dream is to be bold and oversee what is happening to my local municipality

"I've learnt through my community work that just because you are not very educated doesn't mean you must stop dreaming or building yourself up; you mustn't stop taking yourself seriously."

because the ward councillors are deployed by the community to represent us in the government. We women must not quit.

I'd be so happy if one day I woke up to see Lingani Senior Secondary School looking like a high school and not a lower primary school – our children were not sitting outside, whether rain or shine, because there are too few classrooms. Sometimes, there are two schools in one building. One will start in the morning, and the other starts in the afternoon. An NGO wanted to build a school, but the government said they must only build two classrooms. The foundation of the school was built by us parents. Government wanted it demolished because they said it was not proper. We refused. We said, "If you demolish it, what will you replace it with?"

The Freedom Charter said: "The Land will belong to the people". We don't have grazing land for our cattle. *Amasimi akulinywanga*. Now we have to use tractors, not cattle and ploughs like we used to. If you don't have a tractor you have to hire from someone who has one, and that is expensive. My dream is that the government can implement the promises of the past ten years to us rural people. Then women's lives will be better too.

PARTING WORDS TO THE WOMEN AT THE WORKSHOP

Today has changed the way I see my life. Where I stay, I am a leader, but people take me for granted. But from today onwards I am strong. I leave here ripe with ideas. I am going to start a women's forum. I know that when we organise together as women we will breathe spirit and courage into each other. I felt this in the room for the last two days. Being here with other women has given me courage. Where I work it is easy to feel isolated. Things are hard. I know this thing starts in the home,

> " *I don't believe that a woman like me has a better chance in the cities. That is why we must think about our sustainability where we are. We have to at least keep trying* "

before you even go outside. What happens in the communities starts in the home. Sometimes we can feel strong in the community but be weak at home. Today, I say "Enough! We can no longer be ignored as women. We are powerful." As rural women we will play our part. I look forward to the power we can have together as women when we act in solidarity.

UMZALIKAZI BY N.L. ZITHA

Wanyamezel'umama

Naxa sekunzima

Mbon'umzalikazi

ekoba bunzima

Yena akalahli themba

Ngeny'imini wophumelela

Lubone olosizana

Nalo usana emqolo

Noxa ilanga litshisa

Luphakathi kwesithombe

Lulele usana emqolo

Ngamanzi odwa aselwayo

Wanyamezel'umama

Nal'usana emqolo

Yibone inyanda entloko

" The challenge is how to make sure that we also get some of the things we need which can help make our lives easier: electricity, water, good sanitation, good houses, better schools for our children, how to produce our own food, and those things. We have to put our brains together. That is what we are trying to do. "

Lulele usana emqolo

Noxa engenathemba

Layo imbiza eziko

Nanko enyuk'intaba

Lubone olosizana

Luthwel'amanzi entloko

Lulele usana emqolo

Noxa sekunjalo

Uthule uthe cwaka.

Endnotes

1. www.brezi.co.za/index.html
    www.brezi.co.za/keiskammahoek/water.html

"I know everyone says: 'Why do you struggle in the rural areas? Things will never get better. You must go to the cities.' But we are not convinced. We can't all pack up and go to the cities."

Mary Yuin Tal

The Whole World Women's Association was founded because we came to the realisation that … we were experiencing things that could only be expressed by us. We were weary of some man somewhere always representing us and telling the world how we feel and what our needs are. We realised that it was time we started speaking for ourselves, demanding our rights and letting the world know that we were tired of handouts.

I am from Ibalichim, a rural village in the North West province of Cameroon. I am the second child in a family of six. I was raised by my mother and her two sisters after my father and 32 others, including my uncles on my mother's side, were brutally killed in a war between my tribe and the neighbouring Oku tribe. This incident marked my life and changed me forever. It marked the start of my activism and the dream to fight all forms of oppression, war, discrimination and slavery, as well as struggling for the equality of all humankind.

Before working at the Whole World Women's Association, I worked for various human rights organisations, three of which were women and children's organisations. I have a Master's degree in law. I hope to pursue further studies in gender and women's studies. I am a mother of four. I live in Cape Town with my children.

ACTIVISM

I work for an organisation called Whole World Women's Association (WWWA). It is an organisation started by migrant women living in this country as refugees from other African countries with the support of South African women.

WWWA was created because we came to the realisation that, as women, we have unique needs, and that these needs are similar to women's needs across the board. We found there were needs specific to us as mothers, as wives, as single mothers and as girl children. We were experiencing things that could only be expressed by us. We were weary of some man somewhere always representing us and telling the world how we feel and what our needs are. We realised that it was time we started speaking for ourselves, demanding our rights and letting the world know that we were tired of handouts and that we were capable of standing up for ourselves.

> " *The xenophobic attacks have put our work at a level that I did not prepare myself for. I am a mother to other mothers, a counsellor to other counsellors, not just a director as my job describes. I am torn apart dealing with emotions. There are times when I am at a breaking point.* "

WWWA was started as a support group. We did not have a venue where we could meet. We would go to different houses; we would even meet under a tree in the park. We came together to see how, as women, we could support each other. Language was a problem, because we didn't speak Xhosa, or Afrikaans, or English. Most of us speak Swahili, Mbesa, Lingela, Kirwanda, KiCongo or French. When we came together as refugee women, communication was the thing that drew us together. For the first time, I could describe what was happening in my life in a common language: because we could communicate, we trusted each other. Anything shared in the group stayed in the group. No one would laugh at us, criticise us, or make a joke of what we were going through. This is what brought us together.

In 2007 we decided to formally register as an NGO so that the space could continue to exist even if members came and went. If we owned the space, it could grow, not rise or fall with one person. Membership is open to all women of all nationalities, racial and religious backgrounds, especially refugee women and their children. The name is interesting. Women didn't want to put themselves in the box of "refugee" because we had broken out of that box. The fight is not just for refugee women but for all women. And all women relate to this organisation. For us, Whole World Women's Association belongs to all women of the world.

VISION

The vision of our organisation is to identify and empower migrant and refugee women to gain independence and economic and social well-being. The struggles were the same as those faced by South African women, but the difference was that refugee women were disconnected from their social networks and family

" Recently, I sat with women who I know … they came with no self-esteem and could not even introduce themselves. Now they are confident. Now they stand up in crowds and advocate for women's needs. This has given me great courage. "

WHOLE WORLD WOMEN ASSOCIATION

Inspiring women

Our Programs:

Feminist Political Education

leadership training for women and girls

Women's Rights, Human Rights, Refugee Rights

Healing Of Memories Workshops

Human Trafficking Workshops

Gender Equality Workshops

HIV/AIDS Awareness And Management Workshops

Writing and performance skills training

Soup Kitchen

Social Cohesion Workshops

Lobbying and Advocacy.

legal assistance

Because We Care .....

Contact Us on 021 448 5022

41 Salt River Road

Cape Town South Africa

units. We come from backgrounds where family is very important. As African people, we believe in family, especially extended family. Given that we were totally disconnected and isolated, we needed the group to act as our extended family.

CONTEXT

We formally became an NGO in 2007. At this time we struggled for education for our children, for information, rights-based needs, accommodation, access to medical health and a whole range of struggles. In 2008, the political situation in this country changed with the outbreak of xenophobia.

Following the refugee attacks in 2008 – the amount of tears, fear, insecurity, pain, misery, frustration and anger that we experience has been too much to bear. Women who had gained self-esteem were suddenly pushed into a situation of dependency on handouts.

Women did not only lose loved ones in the conflict, but all their belongings and their sense of security. As we speak, women are still struggling to come to terms with their losses. They need someone to be there for them. This has made working in the organisation difficult, and stressful. There are days that I wipe away so many tears that I don't know where to keep myself. I take this home with me and it becomes difficult to separate my home life from my work life.

There is a scarcity of resources of all types, including moral, financial and material resources. The xenophobic attacks have put our work at a level that I did not prepare myself for. I am a mother to other mothers, a counsellor to other counsellors, not just a director as my job describes. I am torn apart dealing with emotions. There are times when I am at a breaking point.

> *Patriarchy ... influences women to act against their own beliefs and against other women.*

On the other hand, there is also great hope and encouragement. For example, the Department of Health has taken a big interest in the lives of refugees and is supporting some of our projects in trying to achieve better health for all living in this country.

The people who come to us for services are mostly refugees and so they have close dealings with the Department of Home Affairs. As far as they are concerned, there is a lot of difficulty accessing any kind of service from this department. It has been difficult for us as an organisation to do anything about it as we do not have control over how this department works. People are saying the Department is filled with corrupt people. The Director there is not aware of these things, so it becomes difficult for him to have control over what is happening. During one of our consultative meetings he advised that some of our people stand and observe in the queues so that this corruption can be controlled.

> *Some women think that we do not need these spaces because they believe they have all they need.*

VICTORIES

The fast growth of the organisation has been a success. The NGO sector struggles to be recognised. Yet, WWWA has taken its place in the South African community, spearheading the fight for refugee women's rights. Our services have touched the hearts of many, including local South African women. Internationally, we are forging our way to join the movements of the women's struggle. I see a bright future for us.

Recently, I sat with women who I know; I know where they come from, how they were when they joined, and where they are now. They came with no self-esteem and could not even introduce themselves. Now they are confident. Now they stand up in crowds and advocate for women's needs. This has given me great courage.

CHALLENGES

How do we get women to have the mindset of helping other women to benefit all? Women sometimes turn around and try to sabotage the same organisation from which they have benefited. This is not just a challenge in the refugee community but in any form of community setting. I have examples of women who immediately discourage other women from participating. Some women think that we do not need these spaces because they believe they have all they need.

In every community you find women like that. I have had the challenge of women who refuse to do something for themselves; when you invite them to a workshop they say, "How much are you going to pay me?" I ask, "How much will the knowledge you gain benefit you?" But they want to know how much Mary is being paid. When you offer transport money for the workshop, but go home in your own car and on your own petrol money, they say, "You gave me R20, but you must have gotten R200!"

The other difficulty is how strong patriarchy is in the community where I work. It influences women to act against their own beliefs and against other women. For example, I was asked, "Do you really have to be a lesbian to be a feminist?" People come from backgrounds with serious patriarchy; it is the religion of these communities. The moment a woman stands up, women will be the first to criticise her, and tell stories about her, like saying that she is a home breaker. My challenge is trying to convince women that being a feminist, that defeating patriarchy is not about being labelled. It is about recognising your needs and the needs of other women. It is about having the space to show what you can do, to have equality, not to be treated like a slave. We come from a society where if you don't have a husband, you can't have respect or dignity; where you are not a woman unless you can have a child; where a woman who has a girl child is despised and hated for not being able to provide a successor for the husband; and where a woman cannot have claim over landed property.

It is a very challenging community as far as patriarchy is concerned. Now we include men in this struggle, the result is that they feel less threatened. They are also the ones who can take the message of equality back to their homes. It's a new strategy; you can hear men saying, "In my house I am trying to bring equality as I learn about it. We share in decision-making, and it is making the life at home better for all because there is less pressure on me to decide and take difficult decisions." Men can see their lives are also improved under this different way of living.

MOVING FORWARD

The key lesson for me in this form of organising is to improve on strategies that work, and change ones we think no longer make sense. We also need to work with other women's movements and learn from people who have been in the same struggle. Learning lessons from other continents is also important; we can't work in isolation.

> " *My challenge is trying to convince women that being a feminist, that defeating patriarchy is not about being labelled. It is about recognising your needs and the needs of other women.* "

"*Communication was the thing that drew us together. For the first time, I could describe what was happening in my life in a common language: Because we could communicate, we trusted each other.*"

Mamy Tladi

I'm from Sebokeng Zone 3, south of Johannesburg, Gauteng. I'm a feminist and have been a community worker since 1989. I've been the Chairperson of the Vaal Community Forum, an affiliate of the Anti-Privatisation Forum (APF), of which I am currently the Chairperson. I'm also the Chairperson of our school governing body and a member of the women's forum, Remmoho. I'm passionate about challenging evictions and privatisation of basic services.

I'm from Sebokeng Zone 3, south of Johannesburg, Gauteng. I'm a feminist and have been a community worker since 1989. I've been the Chairperson of the Vaal Community Forum, an affiliate of the Anti-Privatisation Forum[1] (APF), of which I am currently the Chairperson. I'm also the Chairperson of our school governing body and a member of the women's forum, Remmoho. I'm passionate about challenging evictions and privatisation of basic services, and as a pastor at the Etopian Christian Church, I do political education on equity and women's rights in the church.

ACTIVISM

When we started the Vaal Community Forum we were concerned with the delivery of services of local government, the empty promises from politicians, and evictions. In our township, when a man passes away, the property is usually sold, and the woman and children have nowhere to go. Even if the parents both pass away, the orphans are pushed out. People argue that the title deeds show that the property belonged to the man and woman who passed away, and that the children must find their own houses. Our organisation is fighting this. We believe that the parents have property to leave for their children.

The APF has transport, pamphlets and resources. It is a mother body with 11 affiliates in Vaal, 5 affiliates in the East Rand, ten affiliates in Soweto and four in Tshwane. APF has funds from Oxfam, with a small budget for organisers to teach political skills.

CONTEXT

There are no services in our community. So my question is, how can people owe the municipality R50,000 for services when there are no services? There are

> " *We decided that the children must know what patriarchy is and what it is doing in their lives.* "

no jobs. The councillors don't look and see who is suffering before they evict.

We also started looking after the grandmothers because, in our township, rape of old age women is increasing every day. We get the women together in a daycare centre, and take them home safely. We help with the washing and their medication.

We are also looking at Reconstruction and Development (RDP) houses because we see this as a cause of xenophobia. Local councillors sell RDP houses to refugees who will pay more for them. We believe the councillors have started this thing of xenophobia, and they must now finish and end it.[2] We have had enough. We cannot fight each other because we are all African. We are all poor people struggling to make a life for ourselves. We are not each other's enemy, but we have a common enemy. The system is the enemy.

We took the issue to the APF as our mother body. We demanded action. We went to Alexandra where xenophobic attacks were breaking out. The police were beating refugees and sending them back to the people of Alexandra, who beat them even more. The police station was supposed to be a safe place. But the police would not let the refugees talk to us. We told the police that this was not keeping people safe. We felt we had to invite refugees with us on a "road show" in Alexandra to show that the people we were attacking were also human beings.

Men were attacked and killed in front of their children. We formed a coalition against xenophobia as an APF subcommittee. Representatives from each affected country sit on the subcommittee. We visited Lindela Repatriation Centre,[3] at the end of 2008. We want to shut down Lindela. They take refugees there and treat them like slaves. We want them released, sent home or given a place to stay. While we were there, we saw police trucks full of young children who were saying,

> *We have had enough. We cannot fight each other because we are all African. We are all poor people struggling to make a life for ourselves. We are not each other's enemy, but we have a common enemy. The system is the enemy.*

> **If we do not demand things from our government, we will never have anything on the ground ... The councillors are afraid to come down to address to the community because we are there, in the back, listening, ready to raise our hands when they lie.**

"We are hungry," and, "They beat us." This is still happening because Lindela has not been closed. What action can we take? A pastor from Zimbabwe who is part of the subcommittee was beaten by police and locked up. We protested. They released him and he laid charges against the police. But, there is no truth with our government. The courts say there is no evidence. So, we are trying to take the case over as an organisation. We are still figuring it out.

We have also formed an education subcommittee including youth and parents. Here children learn of their rights in schools. Township principals demand school fees even when their schools are on the list of those that don't charge school fees. As members of APF we put ourselves on school governing bodies. We demanded the schools stop charging people who can't afford fees. In Remmoho, whatever we do we also do for kids. We have a day-care centre. We decided that the children must know what patriarchy is and what it is doing in their lives. Even at APF we didn't realise that we should have a day-care centre during our meetings. When women come with children, the men complain that the child is disturbing them. So we demanded that the APF have a childcare budget for each meeting and event, so that mothers are free to participate.

Another thing we have said is that no one owns the water. Water comes from rain. The government doesn't call the rain, "Come, rain!" They can't take the rain and sell it to the people. We aren't demanding it for free, but we want the councillor to come down to the community to see who can pay and who cannot. Those who can pay are hiding behind those who are not working.

We protest against Eskom, because they lie. How can the pensioner owe the government R60,000 for electricity? We know pensioners should have a discount and

"No one owns the water. Water comes from rain. The government doesn't call the rain, 'Come, rain!' They can't take the rain and sell it to the people."

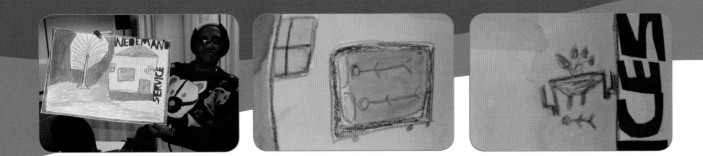

> 66 *We marched on the taxi rank wearing miniskirts to say that a women's body belongs to her. We marched to send a message that if this happens to one woman other women must come to show their support.* 99

yet Eskom admits that this is not happening. Because of the metres, we can't access this "discount" electricity. So we are saying don't buy electricity until the metres are taken out of our homes. We have learned that if we do not demand things from our government, we will never have anything on the ground. With paraffin stoves, kids are dying in fires. We need electricity. The APF struggle expands to the townships. The councillors are afraid to come down to address to the community because we are there, in the back, listening, ready to raise our hands when they lie.

In Welkom, mining families lost their houses when the mines closed down. The mine built the houses, and unless the families paid R4,000 to R6,000 for their "outstanding balances" they would be evicted. But, having lost their jobs on the mine, people had no more money. The councillor then bought the houses for R10 per house. I am still sorting this matter out.

VISION FOR WOMEN

In Remmoho we have made a space for women. We found that women on the ground don't come forward. They have no one to talk to and are living alone. She wants to take an overdose of medication because she cannot live like this. So we made a space to come together and share ideas as women. What we talk about in the room stays in the room. As Remmoho we work with other organisations to gain skills, learn about human rights and for referrals, for instance, when a woman needs counselling.

We also started doing women's leadership training. Usually men are the leaders, and they undermine women, saying she doesn't know how to speak English, or she doesn't know this or that, so you just shut your mouth and don't want to continue.

So we said that it was time for women to stand up to men's harassment. We must stand up against this thing of patriarchy – in our families when our mother-in-law says you musn't tell anyone if your husband fights with you or beats you, when she tells us not to go to the police because he will divorce us. Remmoho shows women how to come forward, how to know their rights and how to fight for them.

As Remmoho we stood up against the taxi driver who harassed the girl at Noord taxi rank.[4] We marched on the taxi rank wearing miniskirts to say that a women's body belongs to her. We marched to send a message that if this happens to one woman other women must come to show their support. In Zulu there is this thing called "ntombinto" where girls wear short skirts, without anything else, in front of men, and they are not raped. So why is this girl supposed to be raped in the township? The (male) taxi drivers said that they would rape us because we should know the "traditions" and that women are not allowed to look like this in Joburg. They then pulled down their pants as we protested.

On 15th June 2009, APF with other organisations will have a night vigil at Hector Peterson Memorial. On 16th June, Youth Day, we will march to police stations to follow-up cases of rape and youth who have been killed. It seems that the African National Congress (ANC) thinks 16th June is for ANC only. We are not going to celebrate 16th June, we are going to mourn. Women will wear black skirts and red t-shirts. The red shows the blood of the children killed on 16th June 1976.

We don't have guns, we are just singing. And yet the police want to catch or kill us for singing for our rights. We wonder what the difference is now – we were shot for protesting during apartheid, we are shot for protesting in democracy too.

> " *We don't have guns, we are just singing. And yet the police want to catch or kill us for singing for our rights. We wonder what the difference is now – we were shot for protesting during apartheid, we are shot for protesting in democracy too.* "

" *When we stand up against men who undermine us, those women in the community who have been undermined get more power. It is not the time of our mothers or grandmothers when they said, 'A man is the head and the woman is the neck.' No a neck cannot move with a head too big.* "

VICTORIES

There have been less evictions since we started organising. We say, "You evict her, we put her back," and, "Arrest us for trespassing, we go to jail for a day, and then we are out."

In some of the partner organisations, there are now women in leadership. I just became national Chairperson of the APF, because women voted me in, even though I was contesting against a man. While the man is educated, knows about the organisations and the politics, as women we say that you must learn by doing. We cannot learn politics and how to handle the organisation without the chance to learn – so the women insisted on me – this is an example of women gluing themselves together.

CHALLENGES

Sometimes women still undermine each other instead of empowering and supporting. Gossiping with men about other women gives men power. Also, to get into leadership positions, many women still feel they need to sleep with men. This also gives men power. Another situation is, while we protested against the Noord taxi driver who harassed Nwabisa, there is an organiser in APF who is accused of raping a woman. Some of the women in our organisation are saying we should support this man, and take his case, "like supporting Zuma". Where are we going then?

In Remmoho, I am facing another big problem. The Chairperson is trying to support the man who raped her, because she is pregnant and he is the father of the child. How do we handle this issue? The media asks me about this, about how I feel about the male organisers. All I can say is that the law must deal with it.

We see leaders who undermine us. Reverends and pastors take teenagers as their wife on the side. If you are a real pastor, then take us forward as a leader. We are looking at you like a picture of who to be. If a leader is corrupt, then the church will go nowhere. Churchwomen have also undermined each other. "Oh, she has a cheap skirt," they say, or, "No socks on Sunday". But, they are coming together, now they give and share, they are working together.

MOVING FORWARD

We must teach women about this thing called patriarchy. When we stand up against men who undermine us, those women in the community who have been undermined get more power. It is not the time of our mothers or grandmothers when they said, "A man is the head and the woman is the neck." No, a neck cannot move with a head too big. We must open our mouths and speak about our experiences. I tell people Moses took the people to Canaan. Some got tired and died and didn't see Canaan, but we will reach the goal, is what I tell them.

> **We must teach women about this thing called patriarchy.**

Endnotes

1. Anti-Privatisation Forum — www.apf.org.za.
2. Hassim, S., Kupe, T. and Worby, E. (eds) (2008) *Go Home or Die Here: Violence, Xenophobia and the Reinvention of Difference in South Africa*, Johannesburg, Wits University Press.
3. A deportation camp on the border of South Africa and Zimbabwe.
4. On Sunday 17th February a 25-year-old women was assaulted when taxi drivers and hawkers at Noord taxi rank in Gauteng tore off her clothes and sexually molested her. It is claimed that she was being taught a lesson for wearing a miniskirt. The Remmoho Women's Forum marched to Noord Street taxi rank on Friday, 29th February 2008, to demand measures be taken to ensure security from this kind of violence against women. Nwabisa Ngcukana told journalists, "As they stripped me they kept shouting that this is 'what I wanted'. Some were sticking their fingers into my vagina while others poured alcohol over my head and called me all sorts of names." She said that instead of Noord taxi rank security staff assisting her, they had mocked her, and asked what she had been thinking, walking around in a miniskirt at a taxi rank. Several women had experienced similar attacks by taxi drivers at Noord.

Shereen Essof

I hold space
for our daydreams & manifestos
for our bold schemes & concrete actions
our rebel laughter & midnight magic
for our circle & our difference.

> **The common thread between all of these struggles and sites is the need for radical structural change based on an understanding that capitalism and patriarchy are mutually reinforcing systems of oppression and they must be dismantled to ensure the emancipation of women and all people.**

I come from many different formations; in Zimbabwe I work with the Feminist Political Education Project (FePep). In South Africa I am part of Feminist Alternatives (FemAL) and have in the last seven years been involved in organising around water access for poor and working-class communities with the Water for All Coalition that began in Mitchell's Plain but attempted to unite communities around Cape Town in the struggle against privatisation of water. I have also been involved in the struggles for better wages and conditions of work at the University of Cape Town through the UCT Workers Support Committee (UCTWSC).

The common thread between all of these struggles and sites is the need for radical structural change based on an understanding that capitalism and patriarchy are mutually reinforcing systems of oppression and they must be dismantled to ensure the emancipation of women and all people.

For the purposes of this interview I would like to talk about the UCTWSC. Established in 2002, the UCTWSC is a group of academics, students and community activists committed to workers' rights to decent and dignified conditions at UCT. The committee works with anyone committed to these goals and is a response to the lack of success by unions and to the more traditional ways of organising and defending workers in outsourced services, as well as failure to address the problems caused by privatisation and outsourcing.

In some ways the UCTWSC has a limited vision with regards to women and all workers. It's a reformist vision for a generic worker to have worker rights and decent and dignified working conditions. The vision provides a foundational set of things to mobilise around. The challenge of being in the UCTWSC and working in a mixed gender space with activists from a range of political traditions

is how do you radicalise the struggle? How do you expose capitalist agendas for what they are? How do you make visible that the "generic worker" is actually a woman worker? How do you integrate the consequences of this analysis into an organising agenda?

For most outsourced workers, women and men, their labour has been feminised. The reproductive work performed by women in the household has been extended by outsourcing into the public sphere of the university, and the work continues to remain invisible, undervalued and underpaid. How do you explain that to workers? How do you work towards a vision that sees outsourcing as a small part of a larger structural system which oppresses people? The challenge, to put it another way, is: UCT workers are fighting for better salaries and working conditions; on return to their homes, they are fighting for access to electricity or water or healthcare or or or… With this understanding it's important, but not enough, to fight for rights and better working conditions at work; the struggle is about more fundamental change. The start of it is to do the work of what I call joining the dots, which will allow the dots to be linked between the household and the workspace and all the other spaces we conduct our work-life. This in itself is an act of resistance because it is in the best interests of oppressive systems to fragment and keep things apart, so that power can be maintained. But to join the dots allows us to see how the capitalist patriarchal systems operate in all of these spaces; how the struggle in each of these spaces is part of the same struggle overall; how my life and socio-economic position is the same as yours; how by coming together we can be strong and make the change that we want.

> *How do you radicalise the struggle? How do you expose capitalist agendas for what they are? How do you make visible that the 'generic worker' is actually a women worker? How do you integrate the consequences of this analysis into an organising agenda?*

THROWING WORKERS TO THE WOLVES

Outsourcing is a direct result of socio-economic and political developments in South Africa. When the ANC-led government decided to adopt GEAR (Growth, Employment and Distribution Plan), it meant that there was a shift from pro-poor policies to the privileging of capital. Certain changes had to be made to allow for the full implementation of neoliberalism. At UCT and other higher education institutions policy changes were implemented to ensure that things run for profit. A big part of this involved the restructuring of labour.

The university was thought of as a knowledge industry, where academic knowledge was given a market-driven significance. Through this process, which sought to create a more efficient university, cleaners, kitchen staff, gardeners, security and maintenance staff became redefined as peripheral or "non-core" to the "business" of the university. In 1999, under the vice chancellorship of Mamphele Ramphele, 267 workers were retrenched, the rest, who were formally employed by UCT, were re-employed by contract companies, like METRO, Supercare, G4 Security amongst others, and the required services were outsourced to these contract companies. All workers experienced salary decreases, loss of benefits and decreased job security.

Workers were thrown to the wolves. Many outsourcing companies do not have clear channels of communication with workers. They have dodgy gender neutral policies on health and safety, leave, benefits and salaries. People are employed on a casual (temporary) rather than permanent basis. Information is controlled by management. Racism and favouritism is rife. This makes things precarious for outsourced workers employed by contract companies.

" It's important, but not enough, to fight for rights and better working conditions at work: the struggle is about more fundamental structural change. "

THE VICTORIES ARE SOMETIMES SMALL AND HAVE TO BE GUARDED

If I have to look at the last seven years of organising we started from a very conscious understanding that there was need to create space for outsourced workers to come together, recognise each other, talk, build solidarity and organise. The experience of a worker in one company is the same as a worker working in another company on another part of UCT's campus, as a worker working in another site. The fact that they are kept apart from each other by the system only serves the purposes of the system. All we did for a long, long time was create a space every week at the same time. Tuesday from 1-2pm. Initially, our gatherings were just UCTWSC people. We met, sat and talked, laughed and shared. We were fierce in our knowledge about the value of creating and holding open such a space. Slowly, slowly workers began to join. We mobilised and more and more workers came to the meetings.

Now seven years later, the space created by the UCTWSC has been formalised into what is called the UCT Workers Forum (WF). This is a victory!

The WF is open to all UCT workers irrespective of union affiliation. The UCTWF is also open to non-union workers. It brings together all workers who work at UCT. It is a platform for all workers to share the problems that they face in different companies that employ them and also discuss solutions to those problems. The UCTWF meets for an hour once a month during lunch break. The UCTWF does not have a recognition agreement with the UCT management and the companies that provide outsourced services at UCT, but through its activities it is recognised by workers and employers and management are aware of its existence.

The UCTWSC continues to provide a range of support activities to UCT workers

> *"Through this organising process women have come to the fore as leaders. In the beginning women who formed the majority at meetings were dominated by a small but vocal male leadership. Over time we now have a vocal and mobilised layer of women's leadership. This is no small thing!"*

UCT WORKERS SUPPORT COMMITTEE

WORKERS CHARTER

Workers demand that all workers, without any loss of pay, benefits or jobs should have the following:

- **A Living Wage**. As a first step, we are supporting the demand of Metro for R3,500pm plus a guaranteed bonus of not less than R3,500 pa.
- **A Secure Job**. Permanent jobs – no casuals
- **Decent, Safe And Healthy Working Conditions**. This includes all the necessary protective clothing, training and safety facilities.
- **Democratic Collective Organisation So That We Can Speak And Act Together.** This includes the right to demonstrate, march, picket, strike without threat or fear of disciplinary measures or dismissal. No –one would be penalized if they refused to cross a picket line, or refused to do the work of a striking worker. Only unionized workers on campus.
- **Open the Books**. No secrets we demand all information.
- **A Safe Place Where We Can Leave Children Who Need Care During Working Hours**
- **Paid Time Off From Work To Learn**
- **Paid Time Off For Union Work And General Meetings**
- **Paid Time Off For Maternity And Paternity Leave And To Look After Sick Children And People**
- **A Decent Pension When You Are Finished Working**. The employer must contribute to the pension.

UCT should immediately pay an allowance to compensate for the disgusting wages of the contractors it has brought onto campus CT should sign a code which says:

- UCT formally accepts the workers set of demands.
- UCT will never sign a contract with any company unless the workers have at least the same wages and conditions.
- UCT will make sure that any contract includes at least the workers set of demands.
- Everyone who is working at UCT and for UCT should be directly employed by UCT, not outside companies and sub-contractors.

LET OUR DEMANDS BE HEARD!

LET OUR VOICES BE HEARD!

and the WF. This has included writing pamphlets in support of workers' struggles at UCT; assisting workers to organise public meetings to highlight the problems of UCT workers; organising direct actions to fight for worker rights; engaging management and outsourced companies to further worker demands; organising winter and summer schools for workers around key areas of the law, rights, the history of struggle, all dependent on where the struggle is at and in support of the agenda at hand. We have embarked on research processes to document particular cases of unfair dismissals, violation of labour law with regards to health and safety and wages by management in order to construct a case and make visible the injustice that happens with impunity. More recently a core group of very dynamic students have come on board through a formation called the UCT Student Worker Alliance.

THE CODE

One of the key activities of the WF with the support of the UCTWSC was developing a unified stance on UCT worker demands that outlines basic demands of all workers at UCT. This document developed in 2004/2005 is known as the Workers Charter.

Intense organising around these demands finally forced the UCT management in 2005 to adopt a code of conduct for outsourced service providers aimed at improving the working conditions of outsourced workers at UCT. This is a victory for workers, even though it does not meet all the demands that workers wanted or may need in the future.

Through this organising process women have come to the fore as leaders. In the beginning women who formed the majority at meetings were dominated by

> " *The gains are fragile, and negotiating and understanding difference and the power inherent in that difference is a challenge, yet is vitally important, when working with a range of people from different political traditions.* "

a small but vocal male leadership. Over time we now have a vocal and mobilised layer of women's leadership. This is no small thing!

But with every gain comes a challenge and working against the negative implementation of the code is one such challenge.

CHALLENGES

There are many more challenges. You make the road as you walk it and things are never perfect or easy. The gains are fragile, and negotiating and understanding difference and the power inherent in that difference is a challenge, yet is vitally important when working with a range of people from different political traditions. Further, when you have workers organise and you have women who are prepared to stand up and fight, and then they get dismissed or transferred and the UCTWSC or WF has no legal standing, it gets difficult and creates vulnerabilities. Every victory has to be claimed and guarded; it is easy for the bosses to claim victories, like the code, as theirs, but it is important to remember that the victories have been won through struggle: workers' struggles.

But perhaps the greatest challenge is to continue to build the alliances, to work across the divides that weaken us, to continue to maintain a space, to continue to ask the necessary and hard questions that wove the struggle from one that is seeking change within the prescribed parameters of the bosses to one that radically shifts things outside of those parameters, to ensure that every person has a decent life, that every person has enough … shift things to a revolutionary struggle underpinned by, for me, feminist principles.

> " *Perhaps the greatest challenge is to continue to build the alliances, to work across the divides that weaken us, to continue to maintain a space and to ask the necessary and hard questions.* "

MOVING FORWARD

Vigilance. Stamina. Creation of autonomous spaces that allow for reflection, strategy, action, reflection. Showing up and being present. A constant bringing back to the fact that outsourcing is gendered, that workers are women. A close reading and re-reading of power. Openness and patience. Process as important as product. Clear articulation and re-articulation of feminist principles. Taking care of yourself and each other in the process of struggle. Laughter. These words, encapsulate some of the lessons.

i hold space

for your ferocity & your tenderness

for your inner warrior & your inner child

for your curiosity & your certainty

for your memories & your tears

i hold space

for your fury & your mercy

for your nerve & your healing

for your greyness & your vivid colours

for your detachment & your concern

i hold space

for our daydreams & manifestos

for our bold schemes & concrete actions

our rebel laughter & midnight magic

for our circle & our difference

> " *We have to shift the parameters of struggle from one that is seeking change within the prescribed parameters of the bosses to one that radically shifts things outside of those parameters … to a revolutionary struggle underpinned, for me, by feminist principles.* "

"The challenge of working in a mixed gender space with activists from a range of political traditions, is how do you expose capitalist agendas for what they are? How do you make visible that the 'generic worker' is actually a woman worker? How do you integrate the consequences of this analysis into organising agendas?"

i hold space

for the movement & the missteps

for the learning lows & hard-earned highs

be we blood

be we comrades

be we homegirls

be we wives

The personal is political

The revolution is feminist

Varsity

THE OFFICIAL STUDENT NEWSPAPER OF THE UNIVERSITY OF CAPE TOWN

5 May 2009 · Volume 68, Number 6 · 021 650 3543 · varsitynewspaper@gmail.com · www.varsitynewspaper.co.za

Long march to workers' rights

PROTESTING - *Students and workers unite to march against outsourcing at UCT. The march ended with a petition handed over to a University official at Bremner.*

BRIAN MULLER

STUDENTS and workers marched side by side last Thursday from Jammie Plaza to Bremner to officially hand over the Workers Letter and the Student Petition to UCT management. Matthew Grant, a member of UCT's Student Worker Alliance (UCTSWA), told VARSITY, "This march is significant because students and workers at UCT will again unite to make UCT a better place for workers... We marched in the spirit of May Day which embodies a hope for all working people and a vision of a better world."

In a statement issued on 2 April, UCTSWA informed VARSITY that workers at UCT "are intimidated by company management, and are not allowed to speak out about their working conditions, are not afforded benefits like medical aid and subsidised tuition fees for their children, and work under pressurised and difficult conditions."

Contrastingly, UCT's mission statement claims to "strive to transcend the legacy of apartheid in South Africa" and "to promote equal opportunity and the full development of human potential".

The Vice Chancellor, Dr Max Price, emailed the student body stating that, "We [UCT] welcome the recent establishment of

UCTSWA and look forward to working with them as well as with other relevant bodies on matters that affect UCT, these being the contractors (service providers) and the people employed by the contractors (employees)".

Outsourcing began at UCT in 1999 causing such a drastic decline in working conditions that in 2004 the Code of Conduct was instated for companies to adhere to in relation to working conditions. This Code did improve working conditions, including an increase of workers' salaries.

UCTSWA claims that this Code was drawn up between UCT management and the companies without consulting any workers, hence workers are still not happy with their conditions.

However, the VC stated in his email that the Code "has drawn praise nationally among both employers and employees". He also stated that "the Code sets out a range of requirements, including matters such as the right to freedom of association and collective bargaining, working conditions, minimum wages, overtime pay, etc. Each company is required to submit a report every six months, indicating their compliance with the code and the employers are given the opportunity to respond."

UCTSWA'S PETITION STATES: WE [THOSE WHO SIGN THE PETITION] ARE ASHAMED TO BELONG TO A UNIVERSITY THAT TOLERATES THE EXPLOITATION OF OTHERS. WE, ALONG WITH THE OUT-SOURCED WORKERS, THEREFORE DEMAND THAT UCT MANAGEMENT:

·*Re-employ all outsourced workers on their terms*

·*Guarantee that all workers currently working at UCT will stay here and that their working conditions will be protected regardless of changes in employment structures*

· *Provide workers with benefits that all staff currently employed by UCT receive e.g. tuition reductions*

·*Provide a minimum wage of R4500.00 per month*

·*End the harassment and intimidation of workers at UCT*

·*Establish a process whereby workers may safely, confidentially and directly communicate problems and issues to UCT management*

Debating race issues

ZERENE HADDAD

LAST Tuesday the Great Debate took place in Jameson Hall. It was the first in a series of initiatives to bring the debate over UCT's Admissions Policy to staff and students on campus. The panel comprised of UCT Academics, a representative from the Department of Education, and four students from different political parties.

The student representatives were Xanthea Limberg from YID, Tende Makofane from SASCO, Ryno Geldenhuys from DASO and Siyaduma Biniza from COPE.

Professor Crain Soudien, acting Deputy Vice-Chancellor, chaired the debate. Each speaker had ten minutes to give their argument, with questions taken from the audience at intervals. The debate was focused on whether race should still be considered the best proxy for disadvantage with regards to UCT's 2011 Admissions policy.

Tende Makofane of SASCO opened the debate. He argued that race should still be used as the principal proxy for disadvantage, citing that UCT had not introduced enough in the way of transformation. He provided statistics to add weight to his argument, stating that, "Although some progress has been made at undergraduate level, with 25,5% of the 2009 student population being African, much is still to be desired at post-graduate level, as reflected by the meagre 12.5% African student constituency; and also with the staff profile, as 88.5% of the University's professors are still white male." These figures are from the UCT Institutional Planning Department (2009).

Professor Benatar, one of the speakers, focused on the issues of redress and diversity, specifically the need to address exactly what "diversity" means in the context of the University.

Continued on page 3...

Wendy Pekeur

I was born on a farm and raised by my grandparents.
This is where I am living still today.

> *As we discussed and did research there was a realisation that there are huge challenges that face farm workers in terms of accessing farms and negotiating better conditions for women. That is why we made a decision to register as a union, to be able to gain benefits for women.*

I come from an organisation called Sikhula Sonke.[1] It means "we grow together". It is a farm workers' trade union. It was established to effect change within the constituency of farm workers. We have been supported by the Women on Farms Project[2] since the 1990s. We thought it would be a social movement. What we've realised is that as women we need to lead efforts for change in our own lives. We never thought it would take the form of a union, but as we discussed and did research into it there was a realisation that there are huge challenges that face farm workers in terms of accessing farms and negotiating better conditions for women. That is why we made a decision to register as a union, to be able to gain benefits for women, such as housing contracts in the names of women, crèche facilities where there are none, increased wages and ownership of land.

And while we discussed what form the movement would take, the debate turned to whether men would be part of it. Legal requirements meant that men had to be included, but we adopted a core principle that women would lead the union. We were born in 2004 on Women's Day, a symbolic day in the history of women in this country. Our registration as a trade union was granted on 10th December 2004, the same year, another important day in the history of South Africa (the day Mandela signed the new Constitution into law in 1996).

VISION

Sikhula Sonke is a vehicle for women's voices to be heard. We facilitate access to certain spaces, for example, parliament or international companies (like Tesco[3]), and ensure that women speak for themselves. We are a home for all workers – migrant, seasonal and temporary workers. We are a school that educates our members.

Through education, you can access many more things and claim your rights.

Our vision is to improve the living and working conditions of our members so that they can exercise their rights and fulfil their needs.

CONTEXT

There are huge problems on farms because of the legacy of apartheid, for example, the legacy of the "dop" system (paying workers in alcohol). The Western Cape has the highest instance of foetal alcohol syndrome in the world. As a result, we adopted a resolution to close down all shebeens on all farms we organise on. We are also acting as a collective against violence against women. It is important for us to work with more people in the farming community and build solidarity to break the divide between what is work and what is personal.

Because literacy levels are low on the farms, our strategy is to move towards doing other kinds of education, looking at audio and video. We have a choir and do education through music. We will have our first CD out by the end of the year. I was the founder of the choir.

We believe that farm workers' children don't need to be farm workers. They can be wine makers, farm owners, doctors and lawyers and that's why we need to change the legacy of alcoholism on the farm.

We are not affiliated to any federation, and especially not the Congress of South African Trade (COSATU). This is because of the tripartite alliance and the fact that it is male dominated. We believe that you have to be outside government in order to be critical of it. We believe that we are a democratic organisation and Sikhula Sonke is a member-controlled organisation. This raises questions about COSATU and their

> " *We are acting as a collective against violence against women. It is important for us to work with more people in the farming community and build solidarity to break the divide between what is work and what is personal.* "

relationship to their members. Do they really represent their members' interests? For us to be strong we don't want to reproduce what COSATU is doing.

There has been a shift in employment patterns. The trend is towards temporary, seasonal and migrant workers, who get low pay, no benefits and no protections. As a union, we have to have policies to organise these vulnerable workers. As a permanent worker, you at least have a home and provident fund. The base of Sikhula Sonke are those who are most marginalised and who do not have secure jobs. It is a challenge for us in terms of sustainability. It also raises a lot of other questions and challenges since it is a difficult environment.

This is not always easy. There is huge migration from the Eastern Cape to the Western Cape. There are race barriers. We try to educate our members that a worker is a worker no matter where you come from. It's the same with xenophobia; our fights are not about each other but against the capitalist system. The capitalist bosses divide the working class based on our differences. It's not easy but we start somewhere and build on that.

VICTORIES

There are now a number of women who have housing contracts; women working as supervisors; and women getting the same benefits and salaries for the same jobs as men. We support the fact that women can be tractor drivers and these are things we discuss when we enter into recognition agreements. On many farms we now have crèche facilities for women, so they know their kids are taken care of.

In the union we have policies that guide elections and last year we passed a resolution that the President and General Secretary will always be women.

> *We are not affiliated with any federation, and especially not COSATU. This is because of the tripartite alliance and the fact that it is male dominated. We believe that you have to be outside government to be critical of it.*

"Sikhula Sonke is a vehicle for women's voices to be heard. We are a home for all workers – migrant, seasonal and temporary workers. We are a school that educates our members. Through education you can access many more things and claim your rights."

People challenge us but we must always be ready to say why this is so and not be defensive in telling men why it has to be like that. If we change things for women we are changing things for everyone in the community. We have proved that with women in leadership we take the "softer issues" that normally fall off the negotiation table and address them first, for example job security, toilets in the orchards and vineyards and paid maternity leave.

> *In the union we have policies that guide elections and last year we passed a resolution that the President and General Secretary will always be women... if we change things for women we are changing things for everyone in the community.*

CHALLENGES

We sometimes feel we don't fit in because we do not understand some of the terms, but we are learning at our own pace.

We have branch elections and 90% of our leadership is women. In one branch a male was elected as Chairperson. On a few farms, male members resigned from Sikhula Sonke because they did not want to be led by women. But when we organise amongst potential members, we make it clear that this is who we are, this is what we stand for and they agree to sign on. But a few years later it changed and they were unhappy about a women-led union. But we are not going to compromise. We will stand by our principles. Men feel threatened by women's leadership. As we grow, the challenges get bigger. We get to areas where men were always the shop stewards and women say they are not able to lead. So you have to build consciousness and deal with internalised oppression, which is a big challenge for us as an organisation.

We also lost three male members due to issues of violence against women in 2008. If male members join Sikhula Sonke they have to sign a declaration that says: "As a male member I hereby refrain myself from any form of violence against women and children or my membership will be terminated."

MOVING FORWARD

We proactively have discussions on the challenges in the organisation. You can't wait until something arises, you have to continuously look at and address issues and take action where appropriate.

As new farms join us, we have to take people through the policies and principles of the organisation so that people understand. We discuss and debate so we don't end up in a situation where it's the opposite of what we want.

Some of the questions we were confronted with are: how inclusive are we in terms of all people in our communities – HIV-positive people, gay and lesbian people, people with disabilities? We had a feminist workshop in 2008 and did a bus trip excercise; we saw that the Afrikaans bus was overloaded while there were no Zulu-speaking leaders. Even though the Western Cape is predominantly Afrikaans, we must have targeted recruitment, so that we organise all workers. We need young and old people, those who are new and come with lots of energy, as well as those with experience.

We are conscious of the power of staff who have training and experience and sometimes you can force your own ideas. But it is something we try to be conscious of and we make it clear that it is not us who are the bosses of the members, but the members who are our bosses.

> " *People challenge us but we must always be ready to say why this is so and not be defensive in telling men why it has to be like that … If male members join Sikhula Sonke they have to sign a declaration that says: 'As a male member I hereby refrain myself from any form of violence against women and children or my membership will be terminated.'* "

LIEFDESPEL

Vlindersag
Streel haar hande die prag
Van twee pieke so trots
As sy telkens met hul bots

Eerbiedig en stil
Het sy haar wense vervul
En sy't haar beloon
Met 'n pryslose kroon

Met die grootste respek
Het sy die tafel gedek
En versadig het sy
Haar in die nektar laat gly

Soos 'n verhaal wat ontvou
Het sy skielik onthou
Om te bemin
Is die geheim om 'n sprokie te begin

So raar
Is hul liefde vir mekaar

"*We are not going to compromise. We will stand by our principles. Men feel threatened by women's leadership.*"

ën fees in die paradys

Die eindpunt, na ën unieke reis

Endnotes

1.   www.wfp.org.za/content/XID3-sikhula_sonke.html.
2.   www.wfp.org.za/.
3.   "Rotten Fruits: Tesco profits While Women Farmworkers Pay," at: www.wfp.org.za/sublist/XID15-research_publications.html, and commented on at: www.guardian.co.uk/business/2009/feb/13/cape-wine-employment-conditions.

" *We get to areas where men were always the shop stewards and women say they are not able to lead. So you have to build consciousness and deal with internalised oppression, which is a big challenge for us as an organisation.* "

Zanele Gladys Mokolo

I'm Zanele Gladys Mokolo from Orange Farm, south of Johannesburg.

" *Water is privatised and they have put up water meters in Orange Farm. Women are fighting this, because we are the ones who feel the pain. We can't just sit and ignore this. We have to stand up and fight this. After the ANC took over government, they introduced the GEAR policy, which is one which led to many of us losing our jobs.* "

I'm a feminist activist and a community developer, working as a community worker since 1990. I am passionate about women's rights and fighting against the privatisation of basic services, the environment and waste management. I am Chairperson of Kganya Women's Consortium and founder of Itsoseng Women's Project.

ACTIVISM

Kganya Women's Consortium is an organisation of women involved in community struggles for basic services, especially for water. Water is privatised and they have put up prepaid water meters in Orange Farm.[1] Women are fighting this, because we are the ones who feel the pain. We can't just sit and ignore this. We have to stand up and fight this.

After the ANC took over government, they introduced the GEAR policy, which is one which led to many of us losing our jobs. So we came together as women to see how we can fight this poverty, and started the project.

These issues really are affecting us as women because women are those who don't have money to buy water. The prepaid meters are like cell phones that need to be recharged. Unemployment is very high in our community. Most of the people are not working. They can't buy electricity or water.

The vision is not only to create community projects, but also to create jobs for ourselves. We want to make women's voices heard. Women's voice is the main vision.

HOW WE ORGANISE OURSELVES

We have public meetings. We address issues in the churches. We also have house meetings, and do graffiti.

We hold monthly meetings for the Women's Consortium. We don't only address the struggle of whatever is happening at the time, we also have women who are affected by domestic violence. These things are discussed. If a woman is involved with other women, and hears their stories, it is easier to disclose these things.

We help each other with resources. For example, someone may use my sewing machine if they don't have one. We also address health issues, for example, encouraging each other to go for pap smears. We even have organisations working with HIV/AIDS.

The water the government says it is giving us is not enough. Sometimes a family of eight uses it, and it is not enough for a month. Sometimes you don't have money to buy the water. Then eight people will use the same water. If children who go to school keep washing themselves with the same water, it is unhealthy. It also kills our culture. When I grew up, if someone was coming to visit you, if you didn't have food you must at least give them a glass of water. We used to just share whatever we had, you can't just give someone a glass of water, you must check the meter first. So we stood up as a Consortium to fight for water.

VICTORIES

We have managed to stop the prepaid water meters in our community. When it started it was a pilot project. They wanted to see whether it would work, only to find it would not. We bypassed the water meters and electricity by connecting cables. We succeeded in stopping the prepaid meters because we did it as a collective. We started to raise our voices.

> *The water the government is giving us is not enough. Sometimes a family of eight uses it, and it is not enough for a month. Sometimes you don't have money to buy the water … If children who go to school have to keep washing themselves with the same water, it is not healthy.*

CHALLENGES

People are divided by political parties, and their attention is taken away from the real struggles facing us… A disappointment is when people from the struggle became part of the ANC government and they started saying we are fighting the ANC government. They don't see that what we are fighting for is not just for us, but for the community at large.

So far we haven't had many disappointments, but the weaknesses are there because we are human beings. People are divided by political parties, and their attention is taken away from the real struggles facing us. We get divided by political parties who don't have our interests at heart.

A disappointment is when people from the struggle became part of the African National Congress (ANC) government they started saying that we are trying to fight the ANC government. They don't see that what we are fighting for is not just for us, but for the community at large.

There is a case of a woman who is married. The husband is working, he does not stay at home permanently. There were allegations against the woman that she is a witch. People from the community started grouping against her. She came to us for help. We went to the Lawyers for Human Rights, and to the police station. Especially in Limpopo, people are burning women who they think are witches. We think the man is having an affair. I don't know if this man does not want the woman any more, or what is happening. The man started organising the people from the community to tell them that she is a witch. He said he has seen her throwing *muti*. He is using his power and community fears of witches. I think all of this is patriarchal. The man feels he can oppress the woman because she does not have an income, but she is surviving in her own way and she is not letting things get her down. It is like he wanted to see her crushed, losing her confidence. It is like it's not enough for him to neglect her, now he wants her to be destroyed. The woman is afraid of disclosing what is happening because this man was abusing her emotionally for years and she was not telling anybody. Because she is not working and the man

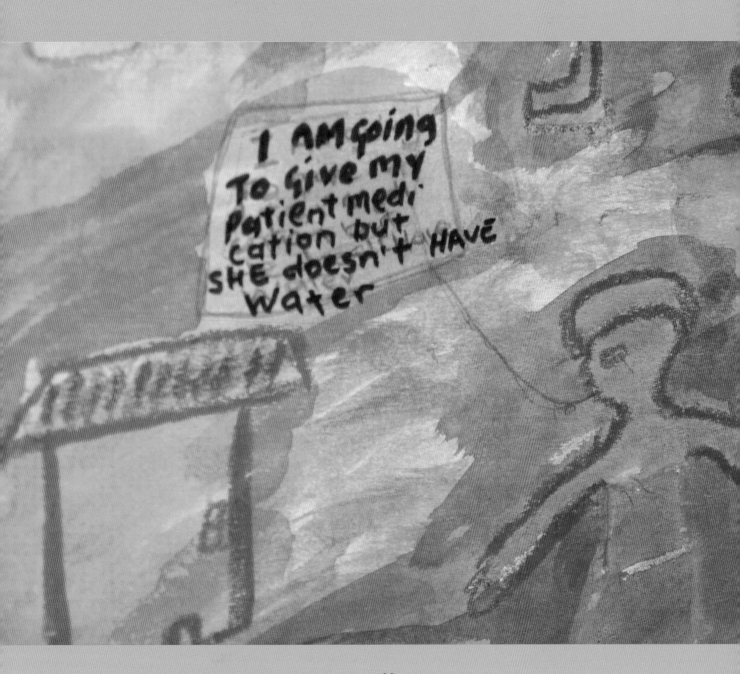

"*Women must keep fighting this patriarchy thing.*"

> *When policies are being implemented people are not consulted. What people know is only to follow the name of the political party, but they don't know the political ideology … We forget sometimes that being members of political parties means demanding they do the right thing for us.*

is working. She is staying there because she does not have a source of income and this man is abusing her because she can't go anywhere. He is using his power against her. We can see the allegations of witchcraft are a lie.

Patriarchy is really affecting us and we have to stand up as women and fight against this. Even if we want to help and support the woman we may not be sure what she is looking for. She needs help but she is afraid of the man because she is not working. And if we say, "We as women are going to fight for you," she may say, "No, leave it." Meanwhile this man is abusing her. It is complicated. But we women must keep fighting this patriarchy thing.

MOVING FORWARD

To mobilise more people to get political education. People on the ground, at the grassroots level, are not aware of issues like privatisation and globalisation. So if people can learn about how the policy of our government affects us, that would help. It is not to say that we don't want our government. We are just dealing with the way things are affecting us.

When policies are being implemented, people are not consulted. What people know is only to follow the name of the political party, but they don't know the political ideology. If people can be taught about political ideologies and how they are affected by the policies which come from these, that would be good. We forget sometimes that being members of political parties means demanding that they do the right thing for us.

Women must stand up and raise their voices. Because privatisation is mostly affecting us as women, because if there is no water or electricity at home, the woman is the one to fetch water, the one to see how to cook for the family, to warm the water, to prepare the food and clean the children. Even if the man is there, everyone will say, "Mom, we want water, we want food."

Women are so brave. When they are together you can never defeat them. But men sometimes feel like they need to be on top. They don't want to give women that space. They feel betrayed if a woman is a leader in the community. It helps to have workshops like this. It is really building us and giving us more power to say, when we go back home, "No, I don't want this." It gives us the power to be self-reliant.

Endnote

1.   Only The Poor Have Pre-paid Water Meters, http://www.alternatives.ca/article975.html.

> **Privatisation is mostly affecting us as women, because if there is no water or electricity at home, the women is the one to fetch water, the one to see how to cook for the family, to warm the water, to prepare the food and clean the children. Even if the man is there, everyone will say, 'Mom, we want water, we want food.'**

Anna Davies-van Es

I am a feminist activist working as a research and education officer at the International Labour and Research Group (ILRIG).

I'm going to talk broadly about an ILRIG[1] project called Building Women's Leadership (BWL). The vision for the project is to build women's activism and leadership within labour and social movements from a feminist perspective combining an analysis of patriarchy and capitalism.

There are two parts to the BWL project. The first part, called Building Women's Activism (BWA) is a monthly women-only public forum that has been running for almost four years. It was created in response to the high levels of sexism in labour and social movements. It aims to create a safe space for women to talk about challenging patriarchy in their organisations, build women's activism and provide solidarity and support between activists within and outside the space in South Africa. Between 20 and 50 women activists attend each month.

The second part is called Building Women's Leadership (BWL). It is a much smaller process that I facilitate. It is an education programme for about 15 activists who come from various organisations. It was formed because of the difficulties of having education that builds knowledge and analysis in a fluid public forum space. At the moment its focus is on a participatory action research process with the group of activists that combines feminist political education around women, public health and research skills.

CONTEXT

Socio-economic developments that have happened over time have informed the work. Neoliberalism and its impact on women as well as increasingly aggressive patriarchy have meant that women are engaged in particular kinds of struggles. At the same time women are involved in organisations that are patriarchal. You tend

" In BWA and BWL we try to understand the context and to politicise women's experiences and to translate that anger into analysis and action. "

to have lots of women in the labour or social movements taking action, but few in the leadership. When women are in leadership positions it is often hard for them to act in women's interests.

Economically women are finding it harder and harder to put food on the table; it's getting more difficult to find decent work. The ways in which society speaks about women has become increasingly anti-women, misogynistic. In BWA and BWL we try to understand this context and to politicise women's experiences and to translate that anger into analysis and action.

THE HIGH POINTS

The successes are really hard to capture because they are not easily recognisable. The process we are involved in does not result in ticking off a list of achieved objectives. You are working with people, not pushing people to achieve certain things. You can have expectations like the women activists will be able to complete certain tasks but I don't think that is the indicator of success. One has to be more fluid in one's analysis of what constitutes success.

A major success is how women who have been involved in BWA and BWL have personally changed, become more articulate, have clearer analysis, connect issues more easily and also take initiatives outside the space. We had originally thought the space would build women's activism in order to strengthen their participation in their organisations and the movements themselves. Although no one has left their organisation and there are signs that organisations are strengthened, they also seem to be taking their struggles to new areas. That might be because the ways in which patriarchy is entrenched in their organisations is too big and the

> *One of the major successes is how women who have been involved in these two spaces have personally changed, become more articulate, have clearer analysis, connect issues more easily and also take initiatives outside the space.*

gains too small so they seek new spaces in which to take action. A success linked to this is that more and more group members from BWL meet independently from ILRIG (without the ILRIG banner and transport money), take action together and provide each other with support.

There are three high points that stand out. The first and most recent has been the presentation and launch of the women and public health research. The group undertook research based on their own experiences and analysis with regards to water and sanitation in their communities. It was one of the first times that people outside of ILRIG actually saw the immense benefit of doing work in this way.

A lot came out of it, for example one woman did research in Tafelsig and has gone on to work with a group of women to complete the survey process for all the houses in the area. The research process has resulted in women in Tafelsig coming together, discussing their issues and taking action. Another example is that one of the women in Overcome Heights has met someone who is going to work with them to find funding to provide adequate sanitation services in that area. That might not be fighting the state or changing the lack of services but it will have a real material impact on their lives, which is so critical.

The second thing that stands out is that there have been various solidarity actions coming out of BWA. These actions were in response to issues raised by group members about the political context. In the case of solidarity with Ogoni Nigerian women it was because one of the woman activists shared the experiences of women in Ogoniland and living outside a refugee camp in Benin. BWA wrote the women a letter and sent education materials: booklets, articles and things we had done as a group (like the definition of patriarchy) so that they could also go

" Feminist political education is a lot more threatening than 'training women leaders'."

THE PERSONAL IS POLITICAL 2008

Forward to the feminist revolution
For liberation from sexism and male domination

JANUARY

m	t	w	t	f	s	s
	1	2	3	4	5	6
7	8	9	10	11	12	13
14	15	16	17	18	19	20
21	22	23	24	25	26	27
28	29	30	31			

FEBRUARY

m	t	w	t	f	s	s
				1	2	3
4	5	6	7	8	9	10
11	12	13	14	15	16	17
18	19	20	21	22	23	24
25	26	27	28	29		

MARCH

m	t	w	t	f	s	s
					1	2
3	4	5	6	7	8	9
10	11	12	13	14	15	16
17	18	19	20	21	22	23
24/31	25	26	27	28	29	30

APRIL

m	t	w	t	f	s	s
	1	2	3	4	5	6
7	8	9	10	11	12	13
14	15	16	17	18	19	20
21	22	23	24	25	26	27
28	29	30				

MAY

m	t	w	t	f	s	s
			1	2	3	4
5	6	7	8	9	10	11
12	13	14	15	16	17	18
19	20	21	22	23	24	25
26	27	28	29	30	31	

JUNE

m	t	w	t	f	s	s
						1
2	3	4	5	6	7	8
9	10	11	12	13	14	15
16	17	18	19	20	21	22
23/30	24	25	26	27	28	29

JULY

m	t	w	t	f	s	s
	1	2	3	4	5	6
7	8	9	10	11	12	13
14	15	16	17	18	19	20
21	22	23	24	25	26	27
28	29	30	31			

AUGUST

m	t	w	t	f	s	s
				1	2	3
4	5	6	7	8	9	10
11	12	13	14	15	16	17
18	19	20	21	22	23	24
25	26	27	28	29	30	31

SEPTEMBER

m	t	w	t	f	s	s
1	2	3	4	5	6	7
8	9	10	11	12	13	14
15	16	17	18	19	20	21
22	23	24	25	26	27	28
29	30					

OCTOBER

m	t	w	t	f	s	s
	1	2	3	4	5	
6	7	8	9	10	11	12
13	14	15	16	17	18	19
20	21	22	23	24	25	26
27	28	29	30	31		

NOVEMBER

m	t	w	t	f	s	s
					1	2
3	4	5	6	7	8	9
10	11	12	13	14	15	16
17	18	19	20	21	22	23
24	25	26	27	28	29	30

DECEMBER

m	t	w	t	f	s	s
1	2	3	4	5	6	7
8	9	10	11	12	13	14
15	16	17	18	19	20	21
22	23	24	25	26	27	28
29	30	31				

ILRIG events
10–12 April – ILRIG 25yr Anniversary
28 Sept – 3 Oct – Globalisation school

Public holidays
1 January – New Year's day | 21 March – Human Rights day | 24 March – Family day | 27 April – Freedom day
28 April – Public holiday | 1 May – Workers' day | 16 June – Youth day | 9 August – National Women's day
24 September – Heritage day | 16 December – Day of Reconciliation | 25 December – Christmas day
26 December – Day of Goodwill

Celebrating ILRIG's 25th year of workers' education

ILRIG

" *A major part of this kind of feminist process is sharing, being honest and creating a safe space in which that can happen. Women activists are asked to come and share their experiences and can share about their personal lives, their work life, their organisational or community activism.* "

through a process of educating themselves and thinking about the world. Part of this was thinking through what it means to provide solidarity from a group who is not in a position to send money or directly provide support. BWA felt it was important to recognise their struggle.

One of the things we also did was taking to the streets in solidarity with women in Zimbabwe. Our actions were motivated by what was happening in Zimbabwe at the time. We had heard stories of women activists being detained, beaten and denied medical treatment. BWA had a discussion and invited Zimbabwean women to share their analysis of what was going on. The group recognised the national boundary between Zimbabwe and South Africa as fictitious and that solidarity could not be stopped. We wrote a solidarity letter to women in Zimbabwe and designed posters of slogans, which we took to the streets in a march from St George's Cathedral to Parliament. It was a march led by women (although there were male comrades supporting) and each woman had been through the process so knew why we were there and each person could engage and respond confidently to passers-by. We also hosted a "welcome brunch" for Zimbabwean women living in Cape Town, based on the recognition that it is not enough to provide solidarity only to women who have stayed in Zimbabwe.

The third high point was the commitment of the various women facilitators involved to thinking through how to make this the best and most feminist process given all the other things going on around us.

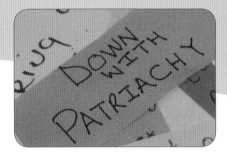 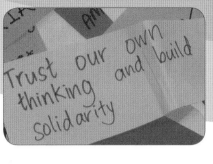 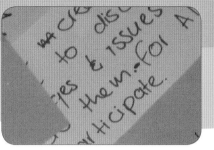

WHEN YOU HAVE TO NEGOTIATE EVERYTHING

One of the difficulties is having to negotiate everything. In these kinds of processes it is individual people who can make or break it. When something changes in your life or in the life of someone in the group, the process can take a different turn. Another weakness, that can also be read as a strength is that you have a hosting NGO with their objectives, a facilitator who works for the NGO but also has their ideas of how things should be done, and a group of women activists coming from a range of organisations with different life experiences. It often falls on the shoulders of the facilitator to negotiate all that.

A major part of this kind of feminist process is sharing, being honest and creating a safe space in which that can happen. Women activists are asked to come and share their experiences and can share about their personal lives, their work life, their organisational or community activism. This forms the basis of the process. On the other hand, when you work at an NGO that is creating the space for that process it is not appropriate to give details on your own struggles and negotiations that might occur within that organisation.

It gets complicated as women have chosen to work together because they have become so close through this process. They associate themselves as BWA or BWL, which is not actually an organisation. It is not a bad thing that the lines get crossed, but it is important to understand why it happens and to be aware of it.

WHAT ARE THE KEY LESSONS IN MOVING FORWARD?

I think the next step for us is to create space for the BWL group to re-evaluate and think strategically about their relationship with ILRIG. Then to build on what has

> " *The group recognised the national boundary between Zimbabwe and South Africa as fictitious and that solidarity could not be stopped.* "

"One of the difficulties is having to negotiate everything … you have a hosting NGO with their objectives, a facilitator who works for the NGO but also has their ideas of how things should be done, and a group of women activists coming from a range of organisations with different life experiences. It often falls on the shoulders of the facilitator to negotiate all that."

been achieved in almost four years of BWA and three years of BWL and bring the activists who have gone through the process to then facilitate and work with new layers. We as an organisation and as facilitators of these types of processes need to continue to be responsive and keep re-analysing the context.

I think for ILRIG it's time to reflect on the amount of time it takes to facilitate these processes and what it means for an organisation to accommodate and support that.

Feminist political education is a lot more threatening than "training women leaders". You have to prepare for/expect backlash. One of the sessions in the BWL course focused on what would our responses be to sexism in our movements. Many of the women have reported that whilst they personally feel more equipped to understand the world and how that impacts on their organisations, they can now see more than before how women are marginalised, and how male agendas prioritised. But this does not always put them in a good position. As a group of BWA women found when volunteering help in response to the xenophobic attacks in 2008 – refusing to make tea can leave you out in the cold as the male activists continue to exclude you.

Endnote

1. www.ilrigsa.org.za.

"BWA is a monthly women-only public forum that has been running for almost four years. It aims to create a safe place for women to talk about challenging patriarchy, build women's activism and provide solidarity…"

Jean Beukes

I'm a grassroots feminist activist. I play an active role in Building Women's Activism (BWA) and Building Women's Leadership (BWL), which are open feminist spaces for women from diverse groupings. I'm also the Treasurer of a refugee organisation called Whole World Women's Association (WWWA). I also participate in the Social Movement Indaba (SMI) and the Freedom of Expression Network (FXN).

I began organising in all the different departments targeting key people. As many started joining, tragedy struck. One of the first workers I had signed up and who had assisted me with organising was shot at point blank range in Nyanga. I was shocked and devastated.

I was born in District Six, and grew up in the Bo-Kaap, better known as the Malay Quarter. My mother was a domestic worker and my father a textile factory worker. I was the fourth out of five children.

In 1972 I got a job at a haberdashery firm, called Newey Goodman. It was opposite Caledon Square Police Station in Cape Town. Our offices were previously occupied by NUSAS, a student organisation. I was the person responsible for collecting the mail and I came across many letters addressed to this organisation; we would throw their mail away. One day I came across a booklet that looked like a dictionary, but in the middle was an article about Frelimo (Mozambican underground movement) that I read. From then on I opened many letters and took the contents home. The content in most cases was banned literature. This, together with the vibrancy and activism I saw on our streets made me more politically aware of what was really going on in our country.

By 1976, things took a ugly turn. I witnessed busloads of police arriving at Caledon Square. They would sit outside on the pavements in their hundreds, later getting into armoured vehicles, like Caspers, etc, to go and do duty in the townships. Cape Town streets errupted with anger. I witnessed cars being set alight in Darling Street and on the parade.

By 1979 I had to leave that job due to sanctions. Our family had to leave the city centre because of the Group Areas Act. We, together with thousands of other families, were moved to Mitchell's Plain, which was very far from the city centre. Thousands of people had to commute long distances every day, including having to transfer to another bus in Manenberg, that would complete the journey to town.

In 1980 I started working for the City Council as a junior clerk/typist. There I became aware of the huge number of evictions and repossessions taking place in Mitchell's Plain. Many people were coerced into buying their own homes and could not afford the rental repayments. What further infuriated me was the fact that many people could not make ends meet. And the City Council refused to take responsibility for the situation.

In 1981/1982 while being active in the Mitchell's Plain Co-ordinating Committee with Theresa Solomons, doing door to door visits with regards to housing, I was paid a visit by the Security Police who came to "visit" in the guise of the South African Revenue Service (SARS). Most of the committee members were warned that day. Fortunately for me, the incident spurred me on.

Later I joined the United Democratic Front (UDF) and was active in the Cape Areas Housing Action Committee (CAHAC), also worked closely with Trevor Manuel in mobilising people on the Cape Flats.

In 1986 I started working for Woolworths at the Woodstock branch as a cashier and stockroom assistant. I later moved to the head office in Adderley Street. I was the first person at my workplace to join the Commercial Catering and Allied Workers Union of South Africa (CCAWUSA). I began organising in all the different departments targeting key people whom I observed carefully. As many started joining, tragedy struck. One of the first workers I had signed up and who had assisted me with organising was shot at point blank range in Nyanga. I was shocked and devastated.

On the day of his funeral, I travelled by train to pay my last respects to his wife and children. As it was a mass funeral the situation was tense and volatile. Only a few workmates managed to atttend as all entrances were blocked. That day shots

> " *I remember management handing me an envelope with a huge increase, which I politely refused, to their utter disbelief. They became furious. They asked me if I want a house and a car. This I also refused. I told management I have all the faith in our workers' wage-negotiating team and I would wait until they informed me of the amount they had settled on.* "

rang out in Nyanga and Gugulethu and I was trapped. His family arranged with a priest to smuggle me out in the back of his car.

I was still an active trade union member, moving between Mitchell's Plain and Gugulethu. Things became so dangerous during the state of emergency I ended up staying in Gugulethu.

In 1987 our union, the Commercial Catering and Allied Workers Union of South Africa (CCAWUSA), split after a violent takeover at our Burns Road offices in Salt River. On the day of the takeover, my life was threatened because I refused to leave the office where our membership files were kept. I told them the only way to get to our membership files was through me, and I wasn't prepared to hand it over without a fight. The majority of our branch executive committee (BEC) were not prepared for a confrontation. I also wanted to see who was prepared to go all the way. The group had already broken into one office, by forcing the locks open and then proceeded to force open the small safety box. It was clear they knew where our monies were being kept. They then took the money to buy food and drinks. Jay Naidoo of CCAWUSA had joined this group, to our utter disgust. When Nick Henwood, COSATU's Regional Secretary at the time, entered the office, I informed him what had taken place. He just ignored me. It was clear COSATU leadership supported this takeover.

A few days later, we informed our membership what had taken place. Workers then decided that they were going to evict them from the office. Workers arrived by truckloads and they were very angry when they heard what had taken place. A group of workers rushed over to me and asked me, "Jean, wys vir ons die varke wat onse geld gesteel het?" I pointed to the office they occupied and the workers

> *We try to encourage women to speak out ... even if they rape us, we must speak about it, and we must challenge it in court.*

"Women, organise! Resist! The master's tools cannot dismantle the master's house! Only we can, through collective action!"

> *Having water meters and a limited amount of water to use means that women are forced to spend their day carrying buckets of water.*

proceeded to evict this group from our office, and they had to literally run for their lives. When I rushed to the window I saw Jay Naidoo on all fours in the street, it looked as if he fell and was struggling to find his glasses that were lying in the street in front of him. The group of workers from Metro Wholesalers in Hanover Park were chasing him with knives.

Later that afternoon I led a group of workers to COSATU's office in Community House, Salt River, where we confronted Nick Henwood about his behaviour towards workers – as the Regional Secretary of COSATU he was not supposed to take sides. The political situation intensified and the situation became dangerous for us as workers. The union had split into two and management took advantage of this. I felt unsafe. I was followed all the time. My children were followed. My flat was bugged, and I was too scared to go out.

Finally, in 1995 my family fell apart from all the pressure. This led to me being attacked and raped. I then moved into a shelter in Westlake with my children. I remained at the shelter for about a year. Life was very hard. I left when my brother sent me enough money to move out and rent a room in Steenberg.

Thereafter two very serious things happened. My daughter was taken by people and she was returned home in the early hours of the next day. I was a total nervous wreck. The police refused to help me. I was also attacked in my flat and fought with this guy for over an hour. I said to myself, "You are not going to die like this." Eventually a neighbour came to my assistance. After this incident and many break-ins in my flat I returned to Mitchell's Plain to live with my mother.

ACTIVISM

Last year I formed a new organisation called Women of Action in Mitchell's Plain. This is a pressure group. For example, if there is rape at a school (or any other issue) we go and demonstrate at the school. We also try to speak to the victim. We try to encourage her to speak out about her experience. We do this so that the community and the person can be empowered. So even if they rape us, we must speak about it, and we must challenge it in court. We have done done nothing wrong.

In Mitchell's Plain, I am also involved in the Women's Sector of the People's Forum. The Women's Network against Women and Child Abuse recently approached me to collaborate with them. I am also part of the recently formed group United Struggles Against Starvation (USAS), which is a broad front made up of working-class organisations, social and labour movements.

Recently we overthrew the patriarchal structures of the Freedom of Expression Network (FXN) and the Social Movements Indaba (SMI). These structures were male dominated for far too long. Our plan of action is to influence others to join us or form alliances with us. The grassroots activists in BWL have proven that through collective action we can succeed to bring about transformation. This has not been easy, it is extremely difficult, yet we have stood together.

Women of Action has also come up with the idea of a television programme where we could expose how the justice system, the media, the education system, religion, culture and tradition supports patriarchy. This collaboration between feminists could advance our struggle for freedom threefold.

> *It is difficult for people from an ANC background to go against the force that they believe got them the job in the first place. Not everybody takes the same revolutionary action.*

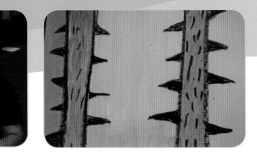

> *The vision of BWA, BWL and Women of Action is to empower women through feminist political education – to undermine, challenge and overthrow patriarchy. It is a journey, built on relationships of trust. The vision is to free women, because as we know women are not free.*

VISION FOR WOMEN

The vision of BWA, BWL and Women of Action is to empower women through feminist political education – to undermine, challenge and overthrow patriarchy. It is a journey, built on relationships of trust. The vision is to free women, because as we know women are not free. We have an economic system in South Africa which is a capitalist patriarchal system. This undermines women. It's a system for men by men. Women carry the burden of household duties, looking after the sick, children and the elderly. Women's bodies are weak from physical labour.

CONTEXT

As you know, the capitalist system is based on the exploitation of women and the poor. Unemployment is high in South Africa. Most women are doing casual labour, and the unpaid or low-paid work that we do in our homes, in our communities and in our organisations is unrecognised and invisible. This is because women's work is not valued by the patriarchal system we live under. This needs to change.

The privatisation of water is a big problem. Having water meters and a limited amount of water to use means that women are forced to spend their day carrying buckets of water. Over time, the amount you carry is unimaginable. This lack of water and inadequate sanitation in the working-class areas poses a major health risk to women, especially if their immune system is compromised. Something as simple as washing becomes stressful, because women do not have enough water to do it all at once. This makes more work for the women and it controls us. Your body becomes tired. As a woman you have no time for leisure because you are constantly busy. You get weak and sick. Every chore, even using the toilet, becomes stressful, because the water is rationed and you have to watch the meter all the time.

VICTORIES

Women in my community in Tafelsig, Mitchell's Plain, are now meeting on a monthly basis. Meetings have grown in popularity because women come to speak to other women in a safe space. People open up and disclose to one another, raise issues and share experiences, for example, water and sanitation. These women were also involved in the formation of the USAS.

USAS held its first protest action at the World Economic Forum on Africa on 10th June 2009 at the Cape Town International Convention Centre. It was a huge success. The aim was to re-unite the working class to come together and unite in response to a lack of leadership from the working-class federation COSATU. COSATU is not seeing to the needs of the workers anymore. It is seeing to the needs of its own pockets. For instance, shop stewards undermine the working class. The management and SACCAWU shop stewards ignore cases of sexual harassment at the workplace. They are not working in the interests of and according to the needs of the working class.

Leadership have lost the plot. Another example is that management and SACCAWU shop stewards in Constantia are in bed together. Both ignore cases of sexual harassment in the workplace. Women are being fired and are being made to pay for the recession. At Pick 'n Pay Constantia women are under attack. Several cases against management lodged by women have come to nought. Cases of

> *The privatisation of water is a big problem. Something as simple as washing becomes stressful, because women do not have enough water to do it all at once. As a woman you have no time for leisure because you are constantly busy. You get weak and sick. Every chore, even using the toilet, becomes stressful, because the water is rationed and you have to watch the meter all the time.*

sexual harassment are swept under the carpet by management. Recently most of the people fired have been women. The unions, SACCAWU and JAMAFU, are not seeing to the needs of their members. When workers became radical and elected a woman shop steward the other shop stewards and management came down on her like a ton of bricks. Within a short period of time she had to resign because the stress was unbearable. So it is clear that COSATU has failed to champion the needs of the working class, especially women workers.

The majority of us are prepared more than ever to dismantle the structures that oppress us as women. We are more united than ever. We have taken action to undermine patriarchy. We have moved the struggle forward through the formation of USAS. This is the start of revolutionary action.

> *People may be involved in activism for years but don't understand how the system of patriarchy works. That is why feminist political education should be like a fire spreading throughout our communities.*

CHALLENGES

We have discovered that not all of us are moving at the same pace. It is difficult for people from an ANC background to go against the force that they believe got them the job in the first place. Not everybody takes the same revolutionary action. For instance, not everybody in the group participated in the formation of USAS.

MOVING FORWARD

We must continue to mobilise our communities. We must do it as a group and all move together as one unit. Unity is strength.

It is important to continue with feminist political education, workshops and public forums. We need to continuously engage women and push women to take action to undermine patriarchy in every sphere of their lives. We need to undermine, challenge and overthrow patriarchy in all its forms.

We have feminist spaces, but some of those spaces are liberal. The difference with our space is that we are radical feminists. It is not just about equality. It is revolutionary. We want all women to be free of the burden of patriarchy.

Women want justice, but how do we access justice when the justice system is patriarchal? We need to create conditions where women can tell their stories: "This happened to me; my husband did this to me for more than 20 years; I was supposed to get 50% of the sale of the house; my husband drove over me; he held a gun to my head; he raped me and nothing happened…"

To move forward we have to be brave once more. We need to step out of our comfort zones. We owe it to all women. Feminist political education has equipped us with the tools to overthrow patriarchy. We have to take very strong action. And we need to move at a very rapid pace. People may be involved in activism for years but don't understand how the system of patriarchy works. That is why feminist political education should be like a fire spreading throughout our communities. We do not have time to waste. The start of the feminist revolution has begun.

We must continue to mobilise our communities. We must do it as a group and all move together as one unit. Unity is strength.

Dorathy (Dora) Leyereue Barry

My desire as a feminist-activist is to contribute to the process that would bring positive change to the Ogoni people in general. In particular, I want to contribute to the process that addresses imbalances, oppression and deprivations that Ogoni women have suffered in the past. I wish to see Ogoni women emancipated in my generation, so that the Ogoni women attain recognition, respect and equality in all spheres of life.

I represent GOWA, the Gbene Ogoni Women Association, which is an affiliate of OSF, the Ogoni Solidarity Forum.[1] OSF came about in 2003, when we were in the Benin Republic, because of the condition of the displaced refugees from Ogoniland, Nigeria.

The leadership of Movement for the Survival of the Ogoni People (MOSOP), the organisation that was formed by the late Ken Saro-Wiwa, had compromised with the Nigerian government. The leadership of MOSOP was not running the organisation according to the original vision. Most of the leaders had an affinity with different political parties, especially the ruling political party, which is against the vision of the Ogoni struggle and MOSOP constitution. The displaced Ogoni refugees as a collective decided to find an alternative, which is how OSF came about.

In 2003, our representative, Comrade Barry Wugale, came to South Africa to create a platform; the organisation got registered as a non-profit effectively from May 2005. That is how we came to be here, representing the voices of the Ogoni people living in Benin. The cardinal aim of the OSF is to create international solidarity and collaboration for the emancipation of the Ogoni ethnic nationality.

GOWA is the organisation I represent and which I have passion for. It was formed as a result of the exploitation of women in Ogoniland. As women, our main occupation is sustenance farming. We sell some of the produce at different markets to get money so that we can send our children to school. When the environment is destroyed, we are faced with food scarcity, which means our children do not go to school. In addition to the effects of a devastated environment, caused by Shell due to oil exploitation, women suffer most in the actual struggle.

> " *GOWA is an association for exiled Ogoni women that aims to empower its members to be free to raise their voices and take their place within the socio-political horizon of Ogoniland.* "

It is women who are raped by the armies. It is women who are forced to cook for the military occupying Ogoniland. It is women who become widows and bear the pain of caring for children whose fathers are killed. It is the girl-child who has to sacrifice her schooling for the boy when a family's source of income is destroyed by oil companies and their agents. It is acceptable because it is commonly believed that the education of the female ends in the kitchen. The numerous sacrifices that Ogoni women made to the struggle are undermined, especially when it comes to positions of leadership and influence in the community. Because of the limited education of women, they don't get much respect.

Women are faced with oppressive cultural practices. For example, you are not supposed to talk in front of a man; you don't own your body, men decide for you; it is an exception rather than a norm for women to speak in public forums; we are not supposed to know more than the men. So these are the conditions women face. In the refugee camp in Benin, women are the ones who are responsible for providing firewood and coal. Women have to go into bushes to look for wood, to make fire and cook. Looking for these means of sustenance, women get raped; some of the women have contracted several infections. And they can't disclose such issues to their partners, so it is a secret that many women carry with them.

There is also the problem of accessing medication. Since we were ejected from the United Nations Refugee camp (we are not recognised as refugees) we don't have access to medication. Many women die during childbirth and due to other preventable diseases. My friend, Dorathy Ikpami, died giving birth to her twins. We took her to a hospital in Ouidah, Benin Republic, and they refused to attend to her. She died in our arms.

> *As women we are the last in everything, such as in education and in leadership roles. We are not recognised. As women, we decided that the system must be challenged. That is how this movement, this space, Gbene Ogoni Women Association (GOWA), was created.*

Women are the last in everything, such as in education and in leadership roles. We are not recognised. As women, we decided that the system must be challenged. That is how this movement, this space, GOWA, was created.

GOWA is an association for exiled Ogoni women that aims to empower its members to be free to raise their voices and take their place within the socio-political horizon of Ogonil and our vision is that women should be empowered. We strive for empowerment in education, political education and "general" education. Empowerment also means that women should be free to raise their voices. But women are not free. Some women still believe that "I am not supposed to do this because I am not a man." Therefore, there is a need to change their mindsets. This is one of our visions.

Another vision is gender equality, in society, at home, between husbands and wives and in leadership, in decision-making, in everything so that we can challenge and overthrow the system of male domination, entirely, in Ogoniland and Africa as a continent.

PARTNERSHIPS

Collaborating with different organisations has helped me a lot, especially Building Women's Activism (BWA) and Building Women's Leadership (BWL). When I first came to BWA I heard other women speaking out and claiming their rights. Then I felt empowered and could stand anywhere to talk about the Ogoni struggle and immediately connected it to the condition of women everywhere.

I cannot fail to mention two persons – Anna and Koni – who helped me to articulate the issue of women's emancipation for the Ogoni and other women

"*Every time I think of the stories and experiences of the women in BWL, I see that all the women are determined, because they have all encountered things that should break them, but they still push on.*"

in the world at large. Anna and Koni, irrespective of their race and educational background, related with me in a friendly manner that motivated me to be focused and to develop myself. The compassion and friendliness they show towards all the members of the BWL boosted my potential.

I have been able to make several contributions which would benefit the entire community of the Ogoni people, and women in particular. I play a key role in a project that strives to generate income in support of the Ogoni women in Benin Republic.

CONTEXT

Benin Republic is a small country and is dependent on Nigeria for sustenance. Because of the language barrier (we do not speak French in Ogoniland) it is difficult to get a job or even to go to school. This also makes it difficult to access resources when organising.

In South Africa, resources have also been a problem. Funding organisations prioritise organisations that are South African-based, working on the plight of South Africans. So we always come at the rear when funding decisions are made. Although we do connect to local struggles, it is not the main focus of our work, therefore raising funds while being in South Africa is a big challenge. But we are struggling and trying to go forward. Hopefully we will get there.

VICTORIES

The first thing is my own empowerment, which I have transferred to other GOWA women in Benin Republic. I communicate with them through email and

> " *The greatest success for the Ogoni struggle is the stopping of Shell for 16 years, which is mostly because of women. From this we can learn that if you unite together as women, nothing is impossible.* "

send publications. So when this publication comes out, I will send it to them also. I encourage them to empower themselves, as demonstrated by South African women.

Another success is the Ken Saro-Wiwa Resource Centre, established through GOWA; we must credit this to the women in GOWA. In addition, we have motivated for women to be included in the leadership; before, it was only men who were in leadership positions. I must give that credit to Comrade Barry Wugale (the OSF Co-ordinator). He encouraged me to seek and acquire knowledge. Comrade Barry always says: "Dora, things should not always be the same; we should not be stuck in the old ways. Equality between men and women is the real way of doing things." Comrade Barry is presently pushing that leadership of the Ogoni should be on a 50/50 basis.

CHALLENGES

Since I came here I have only done voluntary work for the organisation. I don't want to work in a restaurant; I want to work on the issues of my community. Sometimes a project will get funding, and you will get a stipend, maybe R1,000, but it is not every month. If we have funding, it would give me strength. I could then also support the other women in Ogoniland with the basic things they need.

Another weakness is higher education. Political education is not the problem. I wish to further my education, so that I can articulate issues in a proper manner. I feel that sometimes the audience struggle to understand me when I am speaking. I want to be confident, fluent and able to articulate myself clearly. I also wish to develop my writing skill.

> " *The success of the Ogoni women stands out. But women are themselves not free. Some women still believe that 'I am not supposed to do this because I am n ot a man'. Therefore, there is a need to change their mindsets. This is one of our visions.* "

In general, the weakness of GOWA is how we are going to be able to take this knowledge, this experience, back home for the women in Nigeria. They still say women must not do this and that. South Africa is better compared to Ogoniland, where male domination is 100%. In Ogoniland, the majority of the women are very afraid; as such, they accept male domination.

MOVING FORWARD

Every time I think of the stories and experiences of the women in BWL, it strengthens me. Learning about women's stories, such as in this publication, makes me believe anything is possible.

I see that all the women are determined, because they have all encountered things that should break them, but they still push on. It means that they possess positive energy – which is the most important ingredient for a breakthrough in life.

I also link that to the situation of the Ogoni women and their determination, and when, at the peak of our struggle against the re-entry of Shell to take oil from our land, the women organised. The greatest success for the Ogoni struggle is the stopping of Shell for 16 years, which is mostly because of women. From this we can learn that if you unite together as women, nothing is impossible. The success of the Ogoni women stands out; men tried but they didn't succeed. After the killing of Ken Saro-Wiwa and his colleagues, it took the mobilisation of women to be able to stand against the re-entry of Shell into Ogoniland, and it was this resistance of the women that allowed the men to gain strength to continue the struggle.

My involvement in the struggle for women's empowerment has shifted my mind. At BWL and BWA, because it is women only and a free space, I was free to

> *After the killing of Ken Saro-Wiwa and his colleagues it took the mobilisation of women to be able to stand against the re-entry of Shell into Ogoniland, and it was this resistance of the women that allowed the men to gain strength to continue the struggle.*

share my story and I was free to say anything in my own language even if it is not well organised. Most other spaces are dominated by men and I would be thinking about the right grammar, the right words and thinking I will embarrass myself. In these spaces I was free to be myself; that gave me motivation and the love, the sisterhood that I found. I look at them and see my sisters and mothers, and love and respect, faithfulness –all these things that have helped motivate me and help me to shift my mind, my thinking – that thinking I was having before – and to change my mindset.

Endnote

1. Ogoni Solidarity Forum – www.ogoniforum.org.za.

" It is commonly believed that the education of the female ends in the kitchen. The numerous sacrifices that Ogoni women made to the struggle are undermined, especially when it comes to positions of leadership and influence in the community."

PEOPLE OVER PROFI

Ronald Wesso

I am currently active in the Agrarian Reform for Food Sovereignty Campaign. My main interest is in building movements that combine struggles for reforms with struggles for a libertarian revolution against capital, racism, patriarchy and the state.

I work for the Surplus People's Project[1] (SPP) – an NGO that supports rural communities in the Northern and Western Cape and stands for agrarian reform and rural development. It centres the interests and activities of people historically exploited by colonialism, apartheid and now neoliberalism. SPP has been around for quite a while. It started in the 1980s when many anti-apartheid NGOs were established.

SPP was started in response to apartheid's policy of forced removals – that is removals of people that the government, of the time, designated as "surplus people". African people had restricted rights to come into Cape Town and people resisted by setting up informal settlements like Crossroads. They got support from academics and journalists and in that way SPP was established as a research project that kept track of the activities and movement of "surplus people". The focus initially was on urban struggles but it has since shifted to rural and land struggles.

VISION FOR WOMEN

The SPP has shown a willingness and inclination to adopt a radical feminist vision. This means that in our work and everything we do we are trying to keep a track of the role of sexism and patriarchy in the social problems we address. We try to keep the focus on rural women who have been excluded from access to land, services and a decent life.

I think the vision of the organisation can be described as women engaging in farming in a way that centres their own emancipation from all of the various manifestations of patriarchy that we see. So for example, some rural areas have high levels of gender-based violence. Women are more likely to be unemployed or employed in casual low paid jobs. The model of neoliberal agriculture makes it hard for women to escape the poverty and oppression that is prevalent in the rural areas.

> " *In our work and everything we do we try to keep a track of the role of sexism and patriarchy in the social problems we address. We try to keep the focus on rural women who have been excluded from access to land, services and a decent life.* "

CONTEXT

The predominant feature of socio-economic and political developments over the last decade and a half was the country's transition from apartheid to what we have now. What we have now is a constitutional democracy of a capitalist kind with an African National Congress (ANC) government implementing a very uncompromising brand of neoliberalism but still able to rely on its standing as the perceived party of liberation and on its capacity to dispense patronage through the state to maintain itself in power.

This has meant that struggles that were basically rebellions against the social system ended up as disgruntled, but still loyal, ANC supporters protesting particular aspects of the neoliberal approach. As a revolutionary what I try to understand is to what extent people's struggles and actions represent attempts to fix the system, or demand that it be fixed, and to what extent they represent attempts to do away with or subvert the system. Obviously I see my own role as a revolutionary to subvert the system. This places you in tension with people who might be fighting for houses, a fight which you support, but you think the way to get houses is to fix the system, do away with corruption and get better policies in place and so on.

I think it's a pretty universal tension that revolutionaries have to deal with. When you think about your own path you start off trying to fix a particular failing of the social system. So you end up fighting for reforms while arguing for revolution. In my case I've become involved in various struggles for reforms: campaigns for water and electricity delivery to poor communities in Cape Town, struggles for better wages and job security for outsourced workers at the University of Cape Town (UCT), struggles for housing and jobs in a particularly poor and divided community

> *"What we now have is a constitutional democracy of a capitalist kind with an ANC government implementing a very uncompromising brand of neoliberalism but still able to rely on its standing as the perceived party of liberation and on its capacity to dispense patronage through the state to maintain itself in power."*

on the Cape Flats called Delft, and finally this struggle that I am currently involved in, for food sovereignty and agrarian reform.

What I've done in all these is to basically support the efforts of the people to win the things they want and need and also to encourage them to go much further than that. Not to accept in their demands, objectives and dreams the limitations imposed by capitalism, but to go all out to satisfy and express their humanity, which requires a revolution, but also makes a revolution possible.

MY ACTIVIST JOURNEY

It's been a journey for me. My starting point was the activist and political background I came from, which was what people call a vanguardist approach. In this approach, you set up a revolutionary organisation on the basis of a strictly defined and clearly articulated ideology and once set up you send out agents to draw people into your organisation by convincing them to agree to the basic tenets of your ideology. Once you've done enough of that and the group has grown big enough, you will be able to launch a struggle for state power, which puts you in a situation to change society on the basis of your ideology.

I have broken from that approach, which describes 99% of Marxists historically, and begun to believe that that approach is actually a damaging thing for society and especially for the oppressed because it keeps them under the tutelage and power of an elite, which may not be a capitalist or state elite but still an elite, an ideological or party elite.

What I've been trying to figure out is how to do things differently and not just become defined by struggles for reforms, which are good in and of themselves. It's

> *"As a revolutionary what I try to understand is to what extent people's struggles and actions represent attempts to fix the system, or demand that it be fixed, and to what extent they represent attempts to do away with or subvert the system."*

The Right to Agrarian Reform for Food Sovereignty

Obama in, Morobi out

"Piketberg prepares for second mass march against farm evictions"

For immediate release   **20 January 2009**

Whilst Barack Obama will be making history entering the White House amongst much fanfare today, Michael Morobi and his family will also make history – they will most probably leave their white farmhouse silently on Thursday, away from the media spotlight.

Unlike the Obama's, the Morobi's are only another statistic. They will only form part of the more than 2 million people who have been evicted from farms since the inception of the ESTA law. The law gives Pemonia farm owner, Rob Duncan, the right to petition the court to grant him an eviction order that will force Michael Morobi and his family off the farm - effectively resigning them to eke out a living on the rural streets.

But the Morobi's are not alone. The Right to Agrarian Reform for Food Sovereignty Campaign will once again support this destitute farm worker. Towards the end of last year, the campaign has marched through the streets of Piketberg with the first court appearance, invaded commonage land in Vredendal, had a sit-in at the Provincial Land Affairs Offices and had a mass march to Parliament where they handed in a memorandum of demands that would concretely address the demands of the landless and the rural poor.

According to Andries Titus, campaign spokesperson, an expected 150 people, including previously evicted families, those facing evictions, land rights activists from the Hantam Karoo, Namaqualand and the West Coast region, will congregate at the farm at 07h30 on Thursday morning. "We want the rest of the farm workers to see that there is a movement that will take up their demands and to give them confidence to fight for their rights as oppressed and exploited farm workers".

A march to the Piketberg Municipal Offices will ensue where feedback will be demanded from the relevant authorities that accepted the memorandum on November 25, 2008.

Please contact Devine Witbooi on 078 907 2566, Andries Titus on 076 511 6614 or Michael Morobi on 073 818 7066 for more information.

a good thing that people in Mitchell's Plain get water and people in Khayelitsha get electricity and people in Delft houses and outsourced workers at the University of Cape Town decent wages, but that is not in itself revolutionary. It is not going to change the system. So how do you then support these struggles for reforms but not support reformism and encourage people to become revolutionaries, and if you do, do you actually enhance the strength for the struggle for reforms or do you diminish it?

The highlights have been those moments where I could see that the struggle for a particular reform transformed into an encouragement of a revolutionary orientation or movement. There have been many like that where people began to move towards saying we actually have to begin to think about overthrowing the entire system of oppression, starting with the way the system limits our own thinking and our own relationships and practices within our organisations.

An example will be an interesting debate we went through in the struggle at UCT, where outsourced workers were earning a ridiculously low wage. And the debate that we had as a group was how much to demand. Workers were trying to calculate an amount that would give them something and still have some chance to pass through the system and be approved by the bosses. Whereas my close allies and I were arguing that workers should start from what they need even if it means that the system at UCT can't accommodate that. In the beginning it was a very hard thing for workers to accept – they ended up demanding R3,500, which is much more than the R1,200 they were earning but still not enough to live a decent life in South Africa. Over years we worked and worked and more and more people began to question how work is understood and rewarded in South Africa under capitalism. So I guess the highlights were most visible to me in the places where I

> " It's a good thing that people in Mitchell's Plain get water and people in Khayelitsha get electricity and people in Delft houses and outsourced workers at UCT decent wages, but that is not in itself revolutionary. It is not going to change the system. "

spent most of my time – Delft and UCT – where those movements grew beyond the limited group of people and limited scope of demands, objectives and issues they were discussing over the years.

A particular aspect of this in both cases was the development of a feminist focus that went hand in hand with the emergence of a leading layer of women activists from the ranks of the struggles. In the beginning the majority were women but leadership was male, but as years have gone by and women have come to the fore, a conscious feminist focus has developed in both cases, to the extent of replacing the original male leadership.

CHALLENGES

In South Africa there's no visible revolutionary left so there's no reference point. When you begin to argue in spaces like the activist spaces I have referred to for a revolutionary approach to the rewarding of work or towards the question of power within activist organisations you are starting from scratch. It's very hard to find living examples of the revolutionary approaches I am talking about. People know only the approaches of bourgeois society and tend to fall back on what they know. Even if these methods are not compatible with their liberation, they have to use them if they don't have or know workable alternatives. The movements and organisations seen to be left play a particular role here. They are seen as custodians of anti-capitalism but they follow the same approach to intra-organisational power relations and wages, for example, as that of bourgeois society. So the struggles I am talking about as offering the hope of breaking with bourgeois methods all happen outside the mainstream of left organising in unions and socialist parties and groups.

In other words Delft, for instance, is a new township in Cape Town built in the last years and established after apartheid. It does not have a long history of community organising neither does it have strong organisation. At UCT, although there are unions, the unions have organised mainly permanent employed workers; same with rural areas – the rural poor have no strong unions. So, people start organising from a very low base with no offices, no means of communication; they don't know meeting procedures. Instinctively or naturally, they turn to organisations who from their track record are seen as being sympathetic to their cause, like the unions and NGOs, but most of those organisations (if you look at their politics and practices) do not break from the way major institutions of bourgeois society operate.

The UCT unions' approach to the question of wages does not break in a fundamental way from the approach of bourgeois society on the question of wages. In terms of power, unions operate in the same way as the mainstream. It's the same with NGOs and that is a major weakness. People are divided into managers and workers in the same way as in capitalist corporations and states. They sometimes (not often) are called by different titles but office bearers, managers and directors in unions and NGOs also grab more than their fair share of empowering work and decision-making power, just like their counterparts in states and businesses. The fact that people start from a low base is not so much a problem – where else would you start? The weakness is when they start, the people who come on board under the guise of helping push them further back from the goal, imposing bourgeois or authoritarian approaches on the new activists. This is particularly clear when you talk about women. All of these struggles need a strong feminist focus otherwise they can't succeed. But there is no way they are going to get that from the unions and NGOs they end up turning to.

MOVING FORWARD?

If you must distil it into one key lesson, it's don't ever accept any condition that undermines your capacity to decide for yourself and the fulfilment of your needs and potential as a human being. What do I mean by that?

Take the case of UCT workers, there is such a huge temptation to say, "Look, let's accept that this is a big wage increase that is going to leave us better off," but the improvement is going to be temporary. If the acceptance of the wage increase means you are going to slack off and back off on a revolutionary standpoint with relation to work, you are going to end up in the same position before long.

It's a big temptation in all groups of oppressed people to say we are too busy or don't have the skills to run the organisation collectively and not undermine each others' capacity to make decisions for ourselves, so let's just leave this to smaller groups who have the time, energy, skills and that may bring a small improvement. Decisions happen and things move, but in the long term the capacity of the membership to keep control over themselves and their organisation diminishes as the confidence and power of the leadership grows, which feeds into the possibility of that leadership becoming a self-serving elite.

So even if it means going slower, don't ever postpone the task of creating a movement that actually reflects the society that you want. You can't say, "Yes, we want a society free of sexism but we live with male domination in the meantime, because women are not ready to take leadership. Yes, we want a society of emancipated work but we live with demanding better pay for wage slaves so long, because we are not yet ready to take on that struggle." We will only be ready by actually doing it.

> " *Even if it means going slower, don't ever postpone the task of creating a movement that actually reflects the society that you want.* "

Endnote

1.   www.spp.org.za.

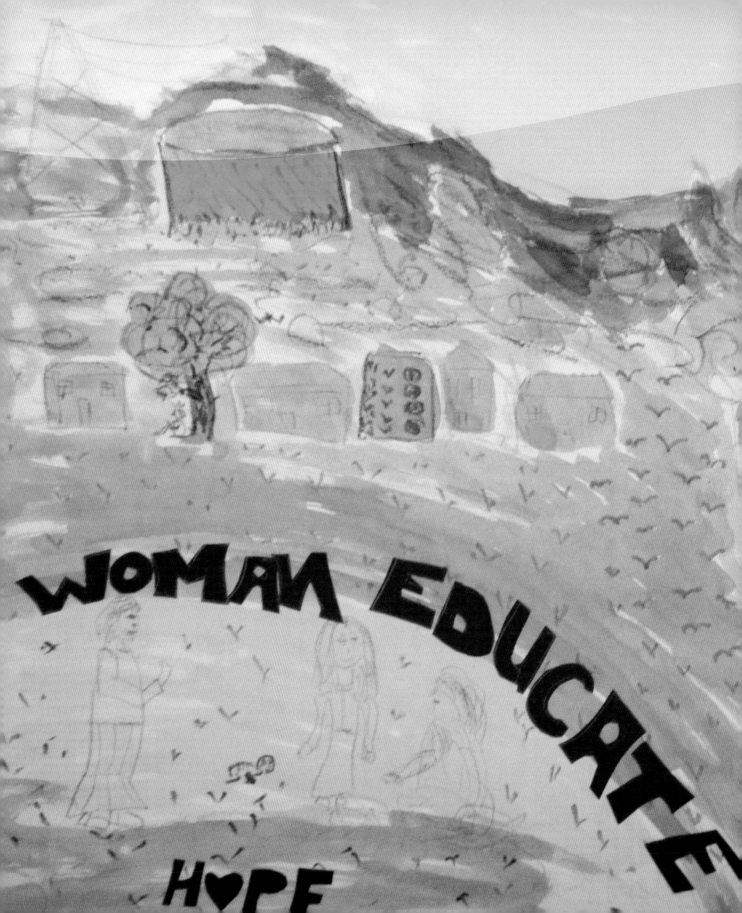

Davine Witbooi

The road was not easy, there have been many downfalls, lots of tears, broken families, but the spirit was there to take the struggle of the poor further. With trust we know we are halfway there, and we are not going to stop until we get what we want. We hold the bucket to catch the tears of our oppressed people, to wet the lands and plant our seeds.

> **"** *... I was trained as a forklift driver... but because I received training and had experience in legal issues and workers' rights, I started working as a political community activist helping people with these kinds of issues.* **"**

My name is Davine Witbooi. My father was married when I was born to another woman. His family didn't want to accept me but he used to visit and so I knew that he was my father. I grew up in Paarl. I was a fifth child. I was raised by my mother and grandmother. My mother was an independent woman and she taught us to be like her and depend on no one but our own strength. During the apartheid era I got involved in politics while I was in high school. In standard 8 I was thrown out of school for getting involved with the United Democratic Front (UDF). So I had to go and work in a factory but carried on being an active member of the UDF, which later became part of the African National Congress (ANC). During this era, many students died and it made me very hard and bitter. I started hating white people because of the system.

ACTIVISM

At KWV[1] I was trained as a forklift driver, and was the first female to acquire this license. After I qualified, I moved to Lutzville on the West Coast.

The first organisation I worked for was concerned with rural development. Because I had received training and had experience in legal issues ranging from labour laws, leadership skills and workers' rights, I started working as a political community activist helping people with these kinds of issues.

CONTEXT

After the democratic elections in South Africa, it became much easier to challenge government policies on service delivery. A platform was also created where people with HIV and AIDS could speak out. NGOs' voices became louder after 1994.

VICTORIES

Seventeen years after being forced out of school, I decided to go back to finish my matric. In 2005 I enrolled for my production manager's course at Damelin College. For the first time in my life I wrote an exam in English. After I qualified I worked as a supervisor and shop steward for a wine company. A couple of years down the line I decided to quit and work for my community, with the NGO Surplus Peoples' Project[2] (SPP) without any remuneration.

I love my work and I feel content because helping other people is something that I love. I became a link between the community and the government. If they had complaints we as the NGO went to them (government) and made them listen to the community's complaints. The government recognised. Our organisation became a model for other similar social movements who experienced non-delivery of services. We mobilised them and helped them to put their structures into place in order for them to have their needs heard by the relevant parties.

We have an agenda and in our meetings we review and formulate action plans. We prioritise by dealing with more pressing issues first, letting the government know that should they fail to meet our demands, we will take action.

> " *Our aim is to fight the neoliberal system of government and to see that land is distributed to black people. After 1994, land distribution was slow and government failed in their obligations.* "

CHALLENGES

After a while, the government officials do not take the marches seriously. They agree to receive the memorandum but when the date comes they do not show their faces.

Another thing is the fact that people do not want to take strike action because they are scared of getting arrested and losing their employment. They do not realise that this is post-1994 and that does not happen anymore. The sad thing is, the South African government only listens when there is strike action.

Also, women do not want to take leadership positions because they say it's a "man's thing". They allow men to dominate them in the workplace, household, community and in organisations. Women trying to challenge patriarchy are not very supportive of each other because they believe it is not part of our culture.

MOVING FORWARD

Look at the bigger picture. There is no box. No boundaries at all. Make a paradigm shift and believe in yourself.

" People in the rural areas are treated unfairly in the new democratic South Africa. Most of them don't know their rights. Our aim is to educate them and help them with all kinds of problems. "

Endnotes

1. Wijnbouwers Vereniging van Zuid-Afrika Bpkt. A wine and alcoholic beverage company in the Western Cape winelands area.
2. Surplus People's Project – www.spp.org.za.

"*The challenges facing small-scale farmers are big with little support from local municipalities.*"

Sipho Mthathi

My name is Sipho Mthathi. My journey to feminism as a political ideology, a way of reading and being in the world, a way of engaging with social reality, of understanding the nature of power, didn't begin in an organisation. It began in my home. For that reason I will talk about where I come from and what I have learnt about from women who came before me.

I come from a family of generations of people who lived by the plough and sickle. Farmworkers and dwellers. Healer women. Indigenous feminists. Social scientists and philosophers who mostly never set foot in a school classroom. A complex family whose historical fabric is testimony to how colonialism and white supremacy dehumanised black people. In the case of black women, how all these, together with the system of patriarchy, took so much more than the anti-colonial, anti-white supremacy struggles cared even to acknowledge.

MY GREAT-GRANDMOTHER

My great-grandmother was a young Xhosa girl when she started working at the farm in which my ancestors lived and worked. She was raped by the farm-owner and a yellow child was born. The Kaffir[1] girl became the one to be ostracised and nearly shot by the farmer's wife for "seducing her husband". Our family did not confront the rapist Baas[2] nor name her violation. The fear of being banished from the farm and never being able to stay or work at another farm again was stronger than their rage at the violation of their child. Nor could they shield her against the social shame ascribed to a woman, a girl, who gave birth to a "bastar" child regardless of the circumstances under which the child came to be. You can say I could not have expected my family to do this at that time and that rape was understood differently then. But this constituted a betrayal by our family, regardless of the racial power relations at play at the time. From then on she spent her time running from her own life. A fugitive in search of a place to birth and hide the evidence of the sexual violence racist white men unleashed with impunity upon black girls and women during the colonial era and its South African version – the apartheid system. She died with neither justice nor inner peace as did others before and after her.

The child she gave birth to was finally adopted, given a name and raised by relatives of relatives and grew up to become a beautiful man and a polygamist. My grandmother was his first wife.

MY GRANDMOTHER

I am granddaughter to a warrior-woman who in many ways embodied the feminist philosophy I have come to embrace; that for a woman, black, peasant, working class, everywhere is a site of struggle and resistance. That caring for each other, acting collectively in defence of each other's dignity makes each and all of us powerful. My feminism and understanding of resistance began in my home as a child under her tutelage, which treated girls and boys the same and made our home into a place of compassion and community for anyone who entered it with respect. She made us all fear for her as she raged at male violence against women and confronted abusive men, sometimes on her own. She insisted that a woman must make sure to have something of her own, whether it's a goat, a chicken, a small piece of land to grow her own food, or else she can never fully appreciate her pride of self.

But my grandmother couldn't read or write so how can I say she taught me about feminism? Of course she did not sit us down and say, "OK, bazukulwana, now I'm going to teach you about patriarchy and feminism."

The essence of her feminism was her refusal to conform to what patriarchy and its supporting social institutions demanded of her as a woman, and in disputing the "natural" position of power the system affords men. She celebrated her indigenous cultural heritage, but confronted hypocrisy in the ways in which some

> *My feminism and understanding of resistance began in my home as a child under her tutelage, which treated girls and boys the same and made our home into a place of compassion and community for anyone who entered it with respect.*

The One in Nine Campaign action on the fourth memorial of the Zuma judgement, 11th May 2010.

normalise oppressive behaviour as "cultural norms" or "our culture", in the ways they cement gendered hierarchies of power in the practice of "culture" to support lies about how men and women should relate, behave or express themselves. She understood also how women become tools through which male power and women's disempowerment is produced and reproduced. Even within the confines of her time and context, she was the first feminist I met.

MY MOTHER

I am daughter to a courageous healer-woman with whom I share a birth place – Salem farm. My mother grew up, started school and was a bright student, until the farmer insisted that my family either handed her over to serve him and his economic enrichment project or leave his farm.[3] In those days black people were rightless tenants and work-horses on white people's farms and defying the farmer's will was a criminal offence punishable by banishment if not physical assault. Ask me if this has changed in our time. My grandmother lost the battle of fighting the system through ensuring that her children got school education, and my mother started working at the farm at age 12. She was later transported to another place 30 minutes away to work at what is today called Stone Crescent – a couple of kilometres from the Settlers' monument, today's primary site of art festivities during the Irhini[4] National Arts Festival. She has spent most of her working life being called a "domestic worker" – a synonym for an underpaid worker with no real labour rights, raising the children and running the household of a wealthy lawyer's family in order to provide food for her own while starving them of attention. Her story is not unique, but in it sits lessons about the politics of black women's labour

> *In those days in South Africa, black people were rightless tenants and work-horses on white people's farms and defying the farm owner was a criminal offence punishable by banishment if not physical assault. Ask me if this has changed in our time.*

in the South African economy. How the bodies of black working-class women have been used to sustain the system of patriarchal capitalism and the white economy. How today black working-class women's bodies and labour sustain the new South Africa's white and black middle-class "nuclear" family economies.

As a first year university student I learnt the word "feminism" and didn't quite understand all the complex academic explanations. But I was struck by how much of feminism's basic tenets had been part of my socialisation, as much as patriarchy had been and continues to be. From the life stories of my ancestor women I learn how true the feminist argument is, that the personal is political. Their life examples also enabled me to discount the nationalistic patriarchal myth which says feminism is an un-African, middle-class women's preserve. Remove the word and insert the principles, women, black women have not only been resisting women's oppression in overt and covert ways, but have been creating alternatives to it throughout history.

MY SOUTH AFRICA

There are many ways in which my South Africa is different from that of the women who came before me. As black people we now have full entitlements by law. White people can't treat us bad and get away with it so easily as they could before. Institutionalised racism has been outlawed, even though the ideology of white supremacy remains and past racial inequities sustain present ones.

I am part of the new South Africa's black middle class with some education and consequent privileges which sometimes make me feel that things are not so bad. I may not be a typical black diamond, but I am a living version of "the South

African dream". Because I exist, it becomes possible to say well, there is more where she comes from, therefore things have really changed. And with that song we can drown the noise of all these houseless, waterless, jobless, justice-less people who are too many to even properly count. It is easy to be co-opted into the socio-political machinery of normalisation, where we overplay progress such that we trivialise the marginalisation of many. Being accountable is a daily struggle.

My South Africa is a place in which the violation of women's bodies to imprint male power, such as was experienced by my great-grandmother, still continues with impunity, despite the good laws and "women-friendly" political gestures.

Those of us who have benefited materially to some extent from the post-apartheid social, political and economic regime consider South Africa a place of hope. But it is also a tragic disappointment for many who struggle to survive and are still told to wait.

I am critical of the superficiality of most post-1994 changes and I find the mantra which says things are far better than they were during apartheid quite unhelpful and in fact serving only to normalise the abnormal. But from my South Africa I have learnt that change is never handed on a platter, it comes only through people's struggles that push and shape the required change. And much change is yet to come for millions of working-class, black, rural, lesbian women and many more people here.

> *Those of us who have benefited materially to some extent from post-apartheid South Africa's social, political and economic regime consider it a place of hope. But it is also a tragic disappointment for many who struggle to survive and are still told to wait.*

STRUGGLES

People speak about wearing many hats; personally I prefer wearing many t-shirts. Among others, I am an active supporter of the work of the One in Nine Campaign. Set up by courageous feminists at a time in 2005 when democratic South Africa's misogynistic colours were laid bare like never before, the Campaign acts in solidarity with women who defy male impunity for sexual violence and the silence and silencing of women in the face of such violations.

For some time I was involved in the HIV and AIDS struggle through my involvement in the Treatment Action Campaign (TAC). TAC is known for many things, but I understood it to be a struggle in resistance to social exclusion, for social justice. It fought to ensure that people living with HIV and AIDS have access to medical care as well as enjoy social recognition as full human beings, citizens with agency, dignity and rights. I joined the struggle for many reasons, including that in the lives of the many people struggling with the realities of HIV and AIDS I saw myself. Mostly young people who look like me were the ones either sick or dying. Then, anti-AIDS medicine cost more than R1,000 a month. Where would a now-unemployed domestic worker get that? The African National Congress government had made it clear that it was not going to take on the world's neoliberal trade regime which saw greedy pharmaceutical companies producing medicine and charging prices that were out of reach for the majority of the people it governed. The struggle for access to affordable AIDS treatment was an unequivocally justifiable, urgent demand. But it was only the beginning of a larger struggle.

From going into homes and sipping tea with mothers and fathers, talking about how they've tried everything to help their child lying in bed in the next room, I got to understand more clearly the essence of post-apartheid South Africa's betrayals of poor and working-class people, the majority of whom are black.

The new South Africa, as I choose to understand it, was built on the ideal of a society which places equal value on the dignity and life of all who live in it. The way the state handled the AIDS epidemic was unjust on a number of levels. Impacted

> *The African National Congress government had made it clear that it was not going to take on the world's neoliberal trade regime which saw greedy pharmaceutical companies producing medicine and charging prices that were out of reach for the majority of the people it governed.*

families and communities struggled, with little state support. Black, working-class mothers, grandmothers and girls paid, still pay, in ways which betray our new South Africa's promises of women's equality.

Sitting in a room full of women, going over the genetic structure of the HIV virus, a woman would ask, "So, how exactly is it that us women get infected more easily and that there are so many of us with HIV?" To say that a woman's vagina tears easily during sex and the men's semen, which contains the virus, remains inside her for a while after was not enough. No biological reason was enough. Something else had to be at play. Then, in the women-only safe spaces we created, one woman after another would talk about how they had been raped as a child or were living in a violent relationship as an adult. Hearing this repeatedly made it clear to me that whilst I was in a movement whose majority membership was men and women who shared material conditions of poverty – unemployment, a ghetto education or none, an inability to pay for privatised water and electricity – addressing the systemic gender power issues was an urgent task.

The work of women's rights activists forced the male-dominated "global AIDS movement" to concede the gendered nature of the HIV and AIDS epidemic. But it still wasn't enough to acknowledge the link between HIV and gender-based violence; gender, poverty and HIV and all these things that some of us in the AIDS movement sang almost robotically, straight out of the mouths of the epidemic's neoliberal technical-language-peddlers.

I could no longer justify to myself why I was not part of a concerted organising effort that afforded women the space to identify their lived experiences as gendered, state their problems and demands in their own terms, through their own voices, craft their own futures without negotiation or apology. So, I proceeded to work with a group of feminists who shared my political disquiet to build Feminist Alternatives.

Now my political activism is informed by a set of central questions: how is this affecting women? Who is this struggle marginalising? What intersecting injustices are we not seeing and addressing? How do we avoid reproducing the very power relations our struggle seeks to change? What vision of the world informs our struggle and how do we translate that in our daily practice?

FEMINIST ALTERNATIVES – OUR EXPERIMENT AT BUILDING A FEMINIST POLITICS FOR CHANGE!

We have used many grandiose concepts to try and explain what we want to achieve through the organising vehicle of FemAL: to dismantle patriarchy; to disturb mainstream understandings of organising. We want a feminist revolution. But the vision is simple. We want a world in which women and all people can be free.

Our starting point is that patriarchy, with all its many guises and supporting systems of injustice, must die and a new politics of power, social organisation and gender norms must emerge. We speak of women not as a homogenous group of neutral victims of the system of male domination. Patriarchy turns us into its own tools. We participate in reproducing and cementing the structures and relations of patriarchal power. As it is a strategy of the system of patriarchal oppression to destroy those who defy it and it is also its strategy to "reward" those who obey it. But many of us have learnt the hard way that the rewards of patriarchy are false because to women, the reward is always accompanied by an even bigger cost. For that reason the spaces we create must be critical of who we are in terms of race, class, sexuality,

> *"Our starting point is that patriarchy, with all its many guises and supporting systems of injustice, must die and a new politics of power, social organisation and gender norms must emerge. We speak of women not as a homogenous group of neutral victims of the system of male domination."*

the choices we make and how we are working together in ways which allow for our full humanity. We want to embark in struggles that bring us the things we need in order to live but also transform power in society. We need new ways of building organisation and which are critical of established struggle cultures. It is not just what we ask for out there from others, it is what we do, the choices we make ourselves which must validate our commitment to a new society. We see FemAL as a space to think about and experiment with these things. We are excited to build this vision because we know so many feminists in our continent and across the world have done so much that we can learn from.

Patriarchy turns us into its own tools, and we participate in reproducing and cementing the structures and relations of patriarchal power.

There are practical problems many women face. So why the somewhat esoteric sounding starting point? Poor and working-class women don't have houses, water, electricity. They are dying from AIDS. They need better sexual and reproductive health services. They need "development". We need more representation in social, economic and political institutions, in government, etc. Rural women have no land and still wrestle with patriarchal "traditional authorities" who see them as minors not entitled to own land or have power. The current system of elite democracy does not allow for the meaningful political participation of "ordinary women". Poverty, disease, etc, is "feminised". Lesbian women are targeted for misogynistic violence including raping them into being "normal women". Women's labour is still not acknowledged and remunerated. Women form the bulk of the unemployed and are often in casualised employment. Social, religious and political hypocrisy still criminalises sex workers – all these things we can be fighting for.

But we have chosen an approach which centres women's realities and from a contextualisation of those realities will emerge ways of engaging with them, from the types and substance of campaigns and other forms of resistance we engage in. The substance of our work will be informed by the substance of women's lives, framed from an unapologetically feminist perspective where class, race, sexual and other intersecting identities will be taken into account.

AND ACTION…SO FAR?

We have engaged in a number of actions as FemAL. As its embryonic version, the Feminist Collective, we organised a regional feminist forum which became a space of co-directed learning and solidarity. Feminist women who have been organising for decades as well as some younger ones from countries including Zambia, Botswana, Zimbabwe, Mozambique, Swaziland, Lesotho and South Africa came together to reflect, analyse and build knowledge collectively around the socio-economic and political contexts of our lives and organise and build solidarity across the fictitious nationalist borders which divide us as people. From there, various relationships of solidarity have evolved and some solidarity actions followed, some of which focused on Zimbabwe.

My most inspiring moment was when Evelyn and Sheila came to address a group of feminist activists at a solidarity event we organised in Cape Town. They spoke articulately of how our hopes have been betrayed by the very liberation movements and leaders who were instrumental in African people's attainment of their liberation from colonial forces. They outlined the ways in which the lived realities of people, women, living in poverty, in Zimbabwe are similar to those of

> *That political parties, regardless of their historical background, past record of integrity or majority status, without radical, independent people's organisation fiercely shaping the change agenda, extending the political space, are gravely, gravely dangerous.*

people, women, living in poverty, here in South Africa. Out of that we could see why patriarchal nationalisms are bad and why we must act in solidarity to smash borders. How critical it is to build and fiercely defend radical people's organisations in post-liberation contexts so as to prevent these "legitimised elite coups" against the people, which is what has happened in many post-liberation contexts including Zimbabwe. Why women must never fool themselves into thinking that when national liberation comes, they will be handed power on a platter by their male comrades, even as they "gave so much to the struggle". That political parties, regardless of their historical background, past record of integrity or majority status, without radical, independent people's organisations fiercely shaping the change agenda, extending the political space, are gravely, gravely dangerous.

Another highlight of our work together so far is this very publication. Collectively we have created knowledge. We are challenging mainstream understandings of what constitutes knowledge and the hierarchies of "knowers" and "knowers-not" that have come to be accepted as normal in the world. We are not just consumers of knowledge generated by academics, researchers or so-called intellectuals about our struggles and conditions of life.

This publication is not just a way of reclaiming a contested space for women not operating in the academic/intellectual sphere, the space of knowledge creation, a space which is itself a site from which to confront patriarchy and the various forms of marginalisation. We are not satisfied with being bodies to toyitoyi in protest marches of the many struggles we are justifiably part of, we want to shape our lives, the society we live in and lead our own struggles. Those of us also active – in struggles from housing to land to electricity to challenging multinational oil companies in the Niger Delta – have understood that we need sharper tools, clearer arguments with which to also make those struggles anti-patriarchal. Patriarchy fights back with brute force and we need tools to deal with the backlash. The FemAL approach incorporates a vigilance on violence, and violence seen in context, with and through its structural underpinnings.

One of the key things we want to do is create autonomous spaces in which we can collectively reflect, sharpen our analysis and understanding of the ways in which patriarchal and linked forms of oppression work, and take action. We call it feminist political education for action. We will borrow from the tools of resistance that feminists from villages to towns, to cities have developed over time and develop new ones which enable us to deal with both the immediate lived realities and needs as well as the larger structural change needed for women to get out of the vicious cycle of fighting just for survival day in and day out.

Endnotes

1. A term which colonialists and racist Afrikaners during apartheid gave a derogatory meaning then used to refer to black people.
2. A term denoting superiority/power and which black people were expected to use when referring to a white person, even if the white person is two years old and the black person is 45.
3. This was the time when policies of labour tenancy were introduced on farms, which meant that you either conformed or the farmer could at a whim chase you out of "his farm".
4. The name given to the place called Grahamstown by the Khoisan people.

HOUSE

CLARE
ABAHLALI BASEMJONDOLO
DURBAN

RANDLES ROAD

ROAD

Tiled house

plastic
ROOF

ALL
Shacks
and
plank
on the
wall
Tiled

300 people using it
men in a que

Toilet que 300 using
1 Toilet

Community
HALL

Abahlali meeting

Zandile Nsibande

I come from Abahlali[1] Women's league. We started it because we felt women needed a separate space in order to have confidence to speak about issues. Many women in informal settlements are already lacking confidence. It becomes worse sometimes when men are around. Women are afraid to speak.

> *We are a movement that speaks. We speak loud and not according to what political parties and comrades like. For that reason we have been criminalised, often called out of order. Our actions are guided by the belief that if being in order means the silence of the poor, then we will always be out of order.*

In the University of Abahlali baseMjondolo (AbM), we take thinking very seriously. We believe the poor do not need politicians or intellectuals to think for them. We speak our demands in our own voices. We developed the concept of the University of Abahlali baseMjondolo because we believe that we cannot build power when we do not develop each other's capacity as the poor. We were also tired of being used by intellectuals who align with us so that they can get information to use to write their big papers and their theories. We use everything at our disposal to build our thinking capacity and communicate our philosophy, our anger. We know that the elites use intellectual words to bully us into handing over our power to them. We have learnt in AbM that to take on elite power we need different things. Different tools. In meetings we teach others about the politics which are relevant to us as the poor, we build political theories from there and not the other way round.

We are a movement which speaks. We speak loud and not according to what political parties and comrades like. For that reason we have been criminalised, often called out of order. But as you will see in our website, our actions are guided by the belief that if being in order means the silence of the poor, then we will always be out of order.

I saw people in denial about AIDS in the community. People believed in traditional healers. I used to help people with home visits. I'd encourage people to go for CD4 counts, and get grants. At the time I was connected with Hope World Wide. I joined the development committee and we formed the Claire Estate Drop-in Centre. It created job opportunities for women, trained women to do home-based care and worked with HIV-positive people and orphans.

At the Centre we give food parcels to orphans waiting for grants. We monitor grant applications. We help people to appeal decisions, to get the documents they need, and educate them on who qualifies for grants. We also give food parcels to people with TB. We deliver school fee exemption forms so children can learn without paying school fees.

From 2006 to 2008 I started working at the Nelson Mandela medical school. I work with CAPRISA doing clinical trials, HIV prevention and microbicides research. Since 2009 I've been working in public health on TB treatment trials. The treatment being used is old, that's why people get MDR-TB and XDR-TB.

ORGANISING

Abahlali started in 2005, when an African National Congress (ANC) councillor replaced the Inkatha Freedom Party (IFP) councillor in Ward 25. We closed the road. We protested. We were in the ANC Branch Executive Committee. We used to sit with "comrade councillor" and nothing would happen. We would go to Ethekweni, *siphuzamatiye sidlamakhekhe*. When we started involving the community in our meetings, then people came.

At Abahlali University we learn community practice. You can have or learn skills without going to school. For example, we teach people about their rights when being evicted. You musn't sign anything when being evicted. You mustn't move without alternative accommodation. We encourage a culture of reading. Old or young.

We do income generation programmes, beadwork, chicken farming and vegetables gardens. We want women to stop relying on men. Even if men don't want to use condoms women don't have to be dependent on them.

> **Men are in denial about things like HIV/AIDS, and when it comes to sexuality issues, they have dictatorship. There is a lot of poverty in the shacks. Many women rely on men because of poverty.**

We fight evictions. Some people don't have IDs, which means that they'll be homeless. Women are then vulnerable, they are raped. Some women will go into relationships so they can find a place to stay. That's also how their children get raped.

We negotiate with the Department of Housing to speed up the housing process. We demand basic services in the shack areas. The municipality now takes shackdwellers' issues seriously.

The councillor's office used to be closed. Now the councillor brings books to the community.

CONTEXT

We struggle with violence against women. We struggle to support each other. Sometimes, as a women, if you intervene in someone's case, a husband can say: "Niyafebana, you are sleeping together, that is why you are helping her."

Men are in denial about things like HIV/AIDS, and when it comes to sexuality issues, they have dictatorship. There is a lot of poverty in the shacks. Many women rely on men because of poverty. That's why we include men in HIV prevention. Men in the settlements think someone with HIV has been loose, slept around. We live in *mjondolos*.[2] Even when houses are built, they are too small. The houses are not dignified. There is no privacy. We don't just want houses; we want houses in which we live with dignity.

VISION

My dream for women in informal settlements: for women to have confidence when it comes to sexual issues; for men to pay attention to the prevention of HIV/AIDS; I want residents of mjondolo to get dignified houses; for parents to have privacy; I want to see the eradication of informal settlements; everything to stop being about "2010".[3]

VICTORIES

We fight poverty. We encourage education. We encourage the University of KwaZulu-Natal to take students from the community. It helps women who are relying on men to stand a chance to get better jobs.

Some women couldn't be active because the men would not let them come to meetings at night. But when the men see things happen, then they are happy and encouraged.

CHALLENGES

The Slums Act encourages evictions.[4] Many people are removed from one *mjondolo* to another *mjondolo*. Not from *mjondolo* to a house.

We lost the case at Ethekweni High Court when we were challenging the Slums Act. Then we went to the Constitutional Court. We asked, "When are you going to eradicate the shacks?"

We don't support any political party. There are challenges because many of our members are also members of political parties. So, many activists got involved in campaigning for political parties during the elections and not coming to meetings.

Abahlali doesn't support issues of gays and lesbians and commercial sex workers. People say culture does not support these, or the issue of abortion. There is great fear that you will be raped if you are a lesbian.

Women are not brave enough. In mass meetings, women don't talk. Then people will complain afterwards. This is hard.

MOVING FORWARD

A platform like Abahlali can help us progress. When we can educate women about their rights, this can help. Women's economic dependence is tied to their ability to exercise choice. For example, when they test for HIV, women are afraid to disclose to their partners. They will say, yes but *siyancenga la*.

Endnotes

1. www.abahlali.org.
2. Shacks.
3. A reference to South Africa's hosting of the 2010 World Cup.
4. http://www.abahlali.org/node/5120.

" A platform like Abahlali can help us progress. When we can educate women about their rights, this can help. "

City in court bid to evict 1

By LENORE OLIVER
Justice Writer

The City of Cape Town has been arguing in the Cape High Court for the eviction of 116 families from a piece of land in Grassy Park that is earmarked for sport and recreational development.

The large group, from the Zille-Raine Heights informal

today, singing freedom songs and waving placards. A large poster with photographs of residents in front of their dwellings was also displayed.

In its papers the city says the families' occupation of the land became unlawful when temporary consent to occupy the property expired in June 2006.

The city said the property had been set aside for the development of sport and recre-

schools and commu the area and that an a about R12 million ha aside over two finan Development was d at the beginning of

According to t families started oc land in March 200

A meeting be Helen Zille, cou housing officials pilot project to f housing for 63 live in deplorab

ok at photographs of residents
viction Picture: SOPHIA STANDER

6 families

in which they could not remai
of In the papers, the city s
set "These events must be
ars. against the backgroun
tart ongoing efforts by (the ci
ar. find solutions for bac
the dwellers in the area, on
g the porary and later per
basis, which entails
housing development
nayor "The planning a
s and mentation of hous
ed in a are seriously comp
nporary set back by perso
s "who to co-operate wi
itions in

Lorraine Heunis

To live in an informal settlement is no joke. Knowing your house is going to flood again, winter after winter. You can fix your shack and lift your foundation, but there is no investment in our future because this is never going to be ours. It is a crime against humanity to not provide adequate housing for the poorest of the poor. How long is long enough? Must we be on the waiting list forever? Living in an informal settlement forever?

"We met once a month in my sitting room. It was mostly women – women who had been on the waiting list for years; women who were renting shacks in the backyards of other people's properties; women who had jobs but who didn't have enough money for bread after paying rent; poor women who had no jobs and survived off grants…"

HISTORY

I was born on 27th August 1969. I am 39 years old. I live in an informal settlement called Civic Road. I have lived here since I was born. I have two children, one foster daughter and one son. I have been married for 14 years. My daughter has recently married and she has a child. So has my son. So I am a grandmother – twice.

My highest education is standard 9 (grade 11). I fell pregnant and didn't finish my education. With the help of my parents, I raised my son. Now and then, the father would contribute to maintenance.

Since leaving school, I have worked one temporary job after another. I first worked for Transmed, a medical aid company, as a tea girl. During the apartheid years, whites were the only ones who could have jobs in the company, even though some of the white women only had standard 7 (grade 9). I volunteered at a nearby school as a teacher's aid. I would also work as a domestic worker for some of the teachers at the same school.

I became a housing activist to fight for myself and for others who are living in the same crisis. To live in an informal settlement is no joke. Knowing your house is going to flood again, winter after winter. You can fix your shack and lift your foundation, but there is no investment in our future because this is never going to be ours.

ACTIVISM

I have lived on an informal settlement for 39 years. Until recently, I lived in the same shack my father had lived in since he was three years old. I decided that things couldn't carry on like this. The fifth generation of our family is being raised in an informal settlement. When are we going to live in a house?[1]

I decided to start a housing organisation. I thought the government would recognise us and give us housing. But they couldn't help us with what we needed. When we went to the municipality, they'd said, "We don't have a house for you yet." One day they said to my father, "We are going to send your file to the local rent office. When your folder gets to the rent office, the next available house will be yours".

But months passed by. I finally walked to the rent office. There was no file. They'd lied and deceived us for all these years. My parents had been told that they were first in line for a house in the early 1980s. My father only received his house in 2007.

It was back in 2005 when I despaired. I was angry. I decided that it was my responsibility to seek God's help and do something. I prayed and fasted about it and the answer that came to me was that I must start a housing project. With no knowledge, no idea what I was going to do, or what I would say to the authorities, I started a housing organisation. We met once a month in my sitting room. It was mostly women – women who had been on the waiting list for years; women who were renting shacks in the backyards of other people's properties; women who had jobs but who didn't have enough money for bread after paying rent; poor women who had no jobs and survived off grants – women who were oppressed because of the system of patriarchy.

We started the project in March 2005. So many women would come to me for help, saying they were being evicted or that their rent was too high. When you rent in somebody's backyard, you pay lots of money every month. But when the owners' bond is finished and their children are grown up and working, the landlord evicts you. People thought I had contacts to get houses, but I was also unemployed, only doing voluntary work at the school when teachers didn't turn

> *...women who were oppressed because of the system of patriarchy.*

up, for R40 a day. My husband wasn't working either; he would get a monthly disability grant. It was really hard.

In January 2006 we decided to organise ourselves, and on the 18th March we occupied council land. It was a Saturday night. I live on Erf 6921 and we were going to occupy the space adjoining us. Occupation was going to start at 8pm. We didn't think about going to jail. The only thing that mattered to us was that women and children who had been living in the cold or as backyard dwellers would get shelter that day – that is all we cared about.

Everyone brought their building materials in wheelbarrows. As the night went on, shacks were standing. The metro police didn't come because they were busy breaking down shacks in a nearby area where another group of people had occupied land to build shacks. When a policeman friend warned us that the police were on their way, some of us stood fast, held hands and prayed as the rest went on with shack building. Shacks of all shapes and sizes were put up. People slept there that night, some of us only at 5am.

At 9am the next morning, a local municipality official came with some metro police. The metro police stood guard while people who worked on nearby farms were brought in to break down the shacks, some on top of the children who were still inside. We didn't realise that they couldn't break down our shacks or evict us without a court order. Shacks were down but we refused to leave the field. We did not know our rights and were very confused, but also very determined to see our action through.

My children, who were both in matric at the time, were assaulted by a policewoman. When my husband came to see what was going on, the metro police assaulted him badly and threw him into the police van. I couldn't help him because I was protecting

> *As women we must be on the lookout for sexism, racism, sexual exploitation, violence against women and other offences. Women shall not be silenced.*

my children. My husband was without shoes. I wanted to know why they were taking him. The police said it was for assaulting a police officer. They also said if I didn't move away from the police van they would take me away too. I went to the police station with my husband's shoes. They then told me he was charged with malicious damage of police property because he had kicked in the police van window – but he had no scratches on his feet. My husband was charged and had to appear in court several times. After a while, the case was withdrawn because there was not enough evidence.

People stayed on the occupied land and slept outside for three weeks. The Homeless People's Crisis Committee came to assist us in the whole procedure. On the day of the evictions, we asked the mayor to come.

Mayor Helen Zille had been in office for two days. She came and stood barefoot on someone's mattress making promises to people. She said, "If you people work with me you will be part of my next pilot project." But today, after many court cases – which are still pending – there is a R13 million sports-field next to the informal settlement where the city put us. The mayor was playing political games with our minds. She was playing with women's lives. We believed that things would be okay after she came.

Out of this situation, we formed ISIS – Informal Settlements in Struggle. There are seven informal settlements and backyard communities which come under the umbrella of ISIS. We are struggling for our housing rights, sanitation and service delivery. We act against evictions.

> " *We have to struggle. We have to organise for housing. We have to know our rights.* "

VISION FOR WOMEN

To empower women so that women should be free from all oppression.

To empower women in all spheres of life, including education and their general living standards. To encourage women to participate in the struggle for freedom, democracy and equality. Women should stand up for themselves, for what they believe is right. As women we must be on the lookout for sexism, racism, sexual exploitation, violence against women and other offences. Women shall not be silenced. Women should always get good information on what they need to know to improve their lives. We will encourage awareness of women's rights and promote women's participation in community decision-making and political processes.

CONTEXT

The mayor has the power. When you are relocated, you have to fit into the area that you are relocated to – think about schools, environment, childcare, safety. One of the areas they wanted to move people to was Happy Valley in Blackheath, 45km away from where the community lives now. Zille is a woman, yet she didn't even think of women's needs. I wonder what she would have done if she was a single mother with no source of income and nowhere to live – what would she have done for herself and her children?

The system works against us. We have to struggle. We have to organise for housing. We have to know our rights. People trusted the government. Some people who used to live with us in Civic Road Informal Settlement did get houses. The rest of us were just hoping and trusting that our houses would come.

But walking back from the rent office that day, to discover that we were not on any waiting list, was enough. Every day. Every year. Different leaks. Floods inside the house with your furniture metres underwater. Getting shocked by bad electricity connections when I try to repair the roof. Using an outside toilet and having to walk knee-deep in

> " *The games played by the politicians must be stopped. We are people, not balls which can be kicked around whenever it is convenient. The government and politicians must start treating us like the citizens we are.* "

water to get there. No. Enough was enough! The struggle had just started all over again. That's when our first housing meeting was held at my shack in Civic Road.

VICTORIES

At the time of our land invasions, my father had started a new family. We built a shack for them within the boundaries of our yard. Someone had called the metro police. They came with seven cars and workers from nearby farms to demolish my father's shack. We phoned the radio stations and sent out press releases to share information about the right to housing and to tell the public what was happening to us. The press highlighted my father's situation. After a few weeks he was given a house with hot water, cold water, two bedrooms, a kitchen and bathroom. After living in an informal settlement for 57 years, my father finally has a house.

CHALLENGES

The games played by the politicians must be stopped. We are people, not balls which can be kicked around whenever it is convenient. The government and politicians must start treating us like the citizens we are. There must be equality. We are not sitting around waiting for handouts. The government promised us a decent life. But we are struggling, and when we try to do something about it, they treat us like criminals. We are not criminals. We are the ones being violated. Criminals are the ones who get big pieces of land to build businesses on and promise jobs that never come. Criminals are politicians who get money and deals from the business people who buy land where people should live.

We are disappointed with the way the court system works. The mayor should go

> *The government promised us a decent life ... when we try to do something about it, they treat us like criminals. We are not criminals. We are the ones being violated. Criminals are the ones who get big pieces of land to build businesses on and promise jobs that never come.*

to court and be held accountable. When the community was forcefully removed from Civic Road Informal Settlements, the new settlement was named after then Mayor Zille and myself, Lorraine: it is called Zille-Raine Heights, which means "pillar of strength". Then Mayor Zille said the people will live there between 10 and 18 months and then go to their permanent land. The interdict came and the eviction order followed.

CHALLENGING STATE POWER

There is a statement that says, "Women and children should be heard, not hurt." But the government together with politicians hurt women and children by not providing a roof over their heads. This is a kind of violence, state violence.

Women suffer. Government should stop abusing them. On the one side, they are promoting rights, while on the other they are taking them away. Some women used to own the houses they were living in, but due to GEAR, many lost their jobs and incomes. They could not afford their houses anymore. Those who were renting could not afford to rent anymore. The government does not have a plan for people in this position. So I can only live on the street or occupy land.

We know it's a crime, our land is not for sale but what can we do if the government won't help us and we have nowhere to go. They are murdering us through this system. We want the government to stop selling our land to private investors and people who come from other countries just to have holiday houses and live in them once or twice a year. It is a crime against humanity to not provide adequate housing for the poorest of the poor. How long is long enough? Must we be on the waiting list forever? Living in an informal settlement forever?

Endnote

1. http://www.capetown.gov.za/en/Pages/Citysantilandinvasionunittostoplandgrabs.aspx.

"I can only live on the street or occupy land. We know it's a crime because the land is not ours, but what can we do if the government won't help us and we have nowhere to go. They are murdering us through this system."

Koni Benson

I currently work with trade unions and social movements looking at the roots, the gendered nature, and the alternatives to the housing crisis today. In search of feminist solidarities, I aspire to collaborative work that centres process, challenges power, and creates new relationships, knowledges and possibilities.

I work as a researcher and educator at the International Labour Research and Information Group in Cape Town (ILRIG). Recently I have taken a step back and have been doing more research than being directly involved in organisations and formations. This was in part an institutional decision, and it also ensured that I completed my PhD dissertation on women's resistance movements against forced removals and for housing in Crossroads from 1975–2005. So it makes sense for me to speak about the possibilities and challenges of feminist, activist and collaborative research.

I have been collecting and studying the life histories of women activists involved in organised resistance in Crossroads, which is located across the road from the Cape Town airport. The first group I'm looking at, the Crossroads Women's Committee, was formed in the mid 1970s. They were resisting forced removals to bantustans. They played a huge role in building and defending Crossroads as the longest standing "squatter camp" under apartheid in Cape Town. They "made history" with substantial victories, as well as faced serious backlash for their efforts. The second example came 20 years later, where in the same place, different women organised the Women's Power Group to raise issues of service delivery in the post-apartheid period. I wanted to know why they organised in women-only formations and what had changed over this 30-year period.

> " *Women lead these struggles because they have the most to lose and feel that no one else is going to solve their problems for them.* "

CONTEXT

The situation of housing in Cape Town is dire. There are 450,000 families on waiting lists and the state builds approximately 11,000 units per year.[1] It's all done at market rates and every year building materials become more expensive and the houses that have been built are cracking and falling apart. This year they are spending almost half of the budget fixing what has already been built. Fifteen years into democracy, development continues to often translate into displacement for shackdwellers. "Temporary" Relocation Areas (TRAs) are set up and people are sent further and further away from where they are living, away from their survival networks, and into these tin towns that even the state admits can only be considered "decent" if they are in fact temporary residences – which is rarely the case.[2]

For example, in Joe Slovo in Langa, people can't afford the rents for houses that will replace their shacks as part of the N2 Gateway project.[3] After a long court case and attempts at direct action to stay, people there are being moved to Delft. They don't want to go, they would rather stay in their shacks in Joe Slovo than move miles away but that would not look good for tourists driving into town along the N2 for the 2010 World Cup.

In Cape Town, with half a million shackdwellers and a 50-year long waiting list, it is clear that you only get what you are organised to take. The formation I have been most involved with is Zille-Raine Heights (ZRH) and their support network Informal Settlements in Struggle (ISIS). Similar to early phases of land occupations, women find themselves without options of where to live decent lives. Most households in ZRH consider themselves woman headed. Women lead these struggles because they have the most to lose and feel that no one else is going to solve their problems for them.

ZRH originally set up shacks in front of an informal settlement called Civic Road. The new mayor at the time, Helen Zille, came and told them that if they moved to a near-by field she would find them proper accommodation in the area. This was all documented by the press.[4] But despite what the mayor said, despite the fact that vans and trucks belonging to the city moved residents to this open field and

Development often translates into displacement for shackdwellers.

> *'Temporary' Relocation Areas (TRAs) are set up and people are sent further and further away from where they are living, away from their survival networks, and into these tin towns that even on admission of the state are not 'decent' unless temporary.*

laid out their shack settlement, eviction notices were served and the people have been demonised as "grabbing land", "illegal occupiers", and "jumping the queue" of the housing waiting list.

The city proposed that ZRH move 40km away to a place cruelly named Happy Valley with the promise of houses. Not only is Happy Valley far from the social networks ZRH depend on for survival, but residents of Happy Valley have lived there for years, some for a decade, without houses. When ZRH representatives asked people there how they would feel if houses were provided to the relocated community, the potential social tensions were clear. So the ZRH community refused to move.

"NO LONGER WAITING": INFORMAL SETTLEMENTS IN STRUGGLE

My historical work on forced removals and gender struggles for house and home resonated with the contemporary situation and the work that I had been doing at ILRIG with informal settlements under threat of "relocation". Together with shackdwellers it was decided that we would focus our ILRIG work to support social movements on the ZRH case. We decided on the media and on research as two ways to support the struggle. The aim was to use the media and create media to get as much political backup as possible. The research was to support the pending eviction court case and was decided and done through a very carefully constructed collaboration that took into consideration who this group of shackdwellers and housing and NGO activists were, where we were each positioned, power dynamics, and agreed upon goals and processes of working.

According to the South African Constitution, under the Prevention of Illegal

“In Cape Town, with half a million shackdwellers and a 50-year-long waiting list, it is clear that you only get what you are organised to take.”

> *Between the neoliberal and sexist norms, people setting up shacks on open fields are called 'land occupiers' and receive little support except from some movements of the working class, which themselves are made up of unemployed people without a solid basis of resources from which to organise.*

Occupation Act, the state can't evict without taking into account "relevant circumstances". That means, circumstances that make people vulnerable, like number of children, women-headed families, disabled people, social grants, etc. Together with the community we pulled in as many support organisations as possible – researchers from the University of Cape Town, Legal Resource Centre, indymedia, and housing activists from across Cape Town. There were representatives of struggles there from Valhalla Park, 8stLaan, Hangberg, Delft, Khayelitsha, and so on. We designed research to survey ZRH and create a map of the circumstances of each household. At the same time we were building a media strategy to profile the people who lived there and build a case against relocation.

The eight-page booklet that was produced opened up into a poster with the slogan "Not From Bad to Worse" which could be handed out in the area and held up at the court house. The court case and appeals are still ongoing.

I am inspired by people who have decided to take things into their own hands. The way we conducted the campaign meant that people could meet other people in the same situation – Cape Town is so geographically segregated and spread out and transport is so expensive – and see what has worked and not worked in order to make some headway. In fact, one of the slogans in the early days of ISIS was just that: "No longer waiting."

THE SMALL BUT IMPORTANT VICTORIES

Collaborative research has meant that the process would in itself be as, if not more, fruitful than the product. It allowed for a kind of solidarity that took into account all the "realities", power dynamics and possible pitfalls when facing such a huge mountain like the housing crisis. Each time we went to learn about the situation of one group under threat of removal, we went with representatives of people in similar situations from across the city. At the time, there were over 50,000 people "earmarked" for "re-location".

The press was dramatising the "mushrooming of 240 shacklands" in Cape Town and reporting on the anticipated arrival of the "red ant" removal squads from Gauteng.[5]

People were isolated. We found organisers and organisation in many of the informal settlements and people had found strategic ways to remain where they were. Some had even been declared legal and received housing or some were still considered illegal yet were connected and set up with electricity. These conversations of possibilities and strategies took place in the face of a sense that yes, the vulnerability is high but that there is such thing as strength in numbers, so despite working with relatively few people and resources, the collaboration was incredibly powerful.

The court case and supporting research was not just relevant to ZRH but important to a range of communities. Interestingly the courts did not accept the research because it was unaccredited, but the information it revealed was repeatedly referred to in the courtroom proceedings by the two lawyers, and the maps and posters received a lot of media attention.

Even though we didn't win the first case, the right to appeal means people in ZRH don't have to move. This is a small but important victory: to not have to move during winter, to not have to try to enrol kids in a new school and buy a new uniform half-way through the year, to be unemployed but know you can survive based on the church and mosque networks of the area you grew up in. This is why people have rather stressed and strained and faced confrontation on an ongoing

" Housing is not an attractive or glamorous struggle to support given the immense size of the housing crisis and the increasing sense of services, like housing or water or electricity, being for sale to those who can afford them. "

basis for the last four years instead of just giving up and moving off the land.

Successfully defending being removed is the tangible benefit or success, but the less visible building blocks have been just as important. Many relationships were built during this process which sustained alliances through intensive periods of relentless struggle and personal and political attacks.[6]

During this time too,[7] the group participated in a meeting organised by Abahlali baseMjondolo, the shackdwellers movement in Durban, in order to comment on the draft Slum Elimination Bill.[8] We could not all go, but in July 2007 we studied the Act and collectively wrote a response that reflected on Cape Town experiences. The movement lost the KZN High Court Case in early 2008, but continued to use various campaign methods and subsequently won the Abahlali appeal to the Constitutional Court, which in October 2009 ruled that sections of the Slum Elimination Act were indeed unconstitutional.[9] These were small but powerful city and nationwide dialogues that contributed to work towards defending people's rights to attempt to shelter themselves and survive. The victory in KZN was indeed an important victory for all South African shackdwellers as the Slum Elimination Act, like the Special Anti Land Invasion and eviction police squads, would have quickly spread to the rest of the provinces.

CHALLENGES

One of the challenges to working collectively and collaboratively is that it takes time and ongoing commitment. People have busy lives and get pulled in different directions. This makes it difficult to sustain intensive organising over a long period of time. The working class is under pressure from all sides and the poor are getting poorer.

There is no well-resourced, politically radical housing organisation working in feminist ways in Cape Town. In the past, there was a wider support network of advice offices and a politics that said removals were wrong. Rents were politicised. Housing struggles were often highlighted as gendered struggles led by black women who had few options when it came to finding legal and decent shelter in the city. Monies were raised by churches and middle- and working-class people on the left to pay legal fees and rents to avoid removals. The mainstream press, like the *Cape Times*, took a progressive stance on housing struggle issues.

Today, it is generally accepted that people pay market rates for houses, that a house is a commodity, an investment. It is widely believed that subsidies are a privilege and people must be patient and then figure out how to pay rents. It is accepted that women take the lead in issues around "the home", but when it comes to housing allocation and leadership, they are often not given space.

Between the neoliberal and sexist norms, people setting up shacks on open fields are called "land occupiers" and receive little support except from some movements of the working class, which themselves are made up of unemployed people without a solid basis of resources from which to organise. In general, housing is not an attractive or glamorous struggle to support given the immense size of the housing crisis and the increasing sense of services, like housing or water or electricity, being for sale to those who can afford them.

THERE ARE NO SHORTCUTS

A feminist collaborative approach challenges us to re-think what solidarity can mean in all arenas of our work in challenging the status quo today. The word

> "One of the challenges to working collectively and collaboratively is that it takes time and ongoing commitment. People have busy lives and get pulled in different directions. This makes it difficult to sustain intensive organising over a long period of time."

collaboration is used all the time to give legitimacy to proposals or projects. It has become another word for "working with", and that can mean a range of things: from teaching someone something in a classroom to partnering with an organisation or service provider. Alternatively, feminist collaborative practice attempts to centre processes, power and positions, and can be one way to enact solidarity. It needs a constant analysis of the situation, where each person/organisation is coming from and where they aim to go. This does not need to be a separate "pre" process, but rather part and parcel of acknowledging the humanity, power, and position of the different people/organisations involved and moving forward from positions of strength and motivation. It takes time. It takes constant questioning. And it takes creativity to imagine and enact ways of moving forward that are good for both the means and the ends.

Endnotes

1. Aziz Hartley, "Cape Town housing crisis reaches new heights," *Cape Times*, 14 March 2007.
2. City of Cape Town, "Update on Delft Temporary Relocation Area ('Blikkiesdorp')," Media Statement, 3 May 2009.
3. Ella Smook, "Report slams running of N2 Gateway project," *Cape Argus*, 1 May 2009; Dianne Hawker, "Joe Slovo residents fight eviction notices," *Cape Times*, 25 September 2007.
4. Lenore Oliver, "City in court bid to evict 116 families," *Cape Argus*, 30 May 2007; Lenore Oliver, "Families fight city eviction bid: Grassy Park dwellers protest at court," *Cape Argus*, 31 May 2007; Christa Prinsloo, "Zille Must Explain, Court Verdict Pending, Nothing Happy in Valley," *Die Son*, 31 May 2007.
5. Murray Williams, "Cape shacklands mushroom to 240," *Cape Argus*, 5 March 2007; Myolisi Gophe, "Controversial Red Ants marching to Cape Town," *Cape Argus*, 18 November 2006.
6. Kobi Benson, "Collaborative Research in Conversation," *Feminist Africa*, Special Issue no. 13, October/November 2009.
7. Beginning of 2007.
8. www.abahlali.org/node/1319.
9. en.wikipedia.org/KZN_Slums_Act.

"*Yes, the vulnerability remains high, but there is such thing as strength in numbers, so despite working with relatively few people and resources, the collaboration was incredibly powerful.*"

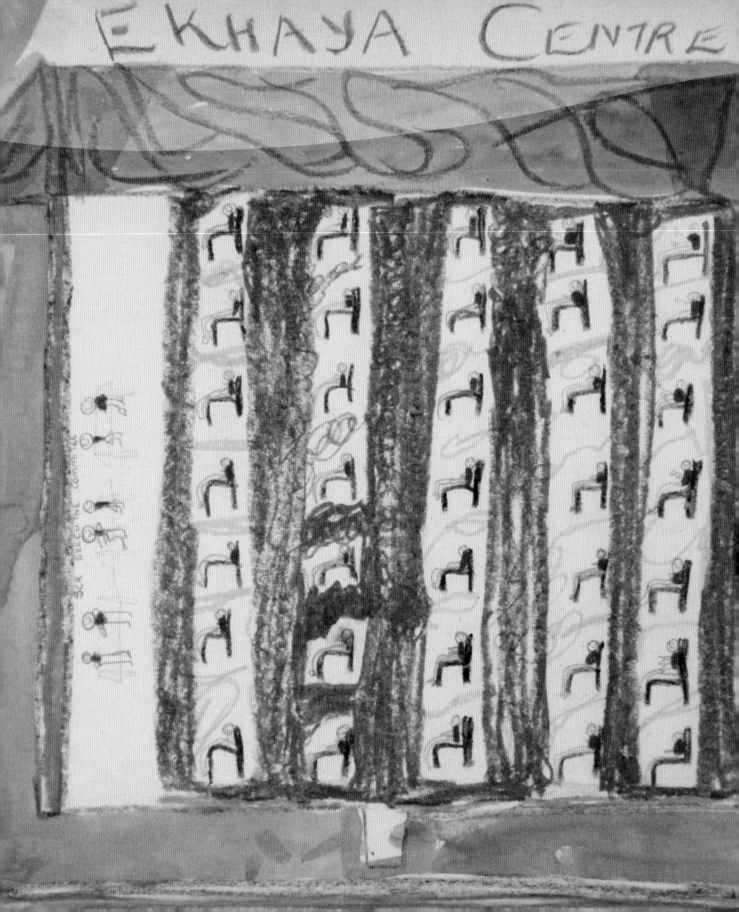

Virginia Setshedi

My name is Virginia Magwaza Setshedi. I started my activism when I was at Khanya College. The education provided there made us feel responsible to be agents of change. I started being involved in community issues. If a streetlight is broken, I'll be at the forefront of trying to fix it.

I was doing my first year at Wits[1] during the introduction of a new macroeconomic policy in the country. This also affected the way the university was run; people were fired because of outsourcing. We were interested in bringing community issues and student issues together. The South African Students Congress (SASCO) gave me an opportunity to change things, even in the communities.

The new neoliberal framework of Growth, Employment and Redistribution (GEAR) led to the privatisation of state assets and services. Eskom was about to be privatised. Then households' electricity started being cut off.

Through my Khanya and SASCO experience, I organised a community meeting to talk about electricity. People had huge debts. I'd call people into our yard and we'd discuss issues around electricity cut-offs and plan what to do. This led to the formation of the Diepkloof Concerned Residents (DCR) organisation.

Within the coalition we started a campaign called the "Women and Water Campaign". It is still a new campaign; we see it as very important. We don't look specifically at the problems experienced by women – women as runners of households who need to use water more. We want to demystify things. We want to have women work with workers in the South African Municipal Workers Union (SAMWU), to be included in issues of water management. In every struggle, women are affected. Every struggle is a woman's struggle.

> " *I organised a community meeting to talk about electricity. People had huge debts. I'd call people into our yard and we'd discuss issues around electricity cut-offs and plan what to do.* "

CHALLENGES

I want to show why it's difficult for a woman to be an organiser. At the time I became an organiser, I was a newlywed. I was young. There were older people who had been in the struggle – in the African National Congress (ANC) or the Pan African Congress

(PAC) who considered themselves more experienced than me. They thought I had good ideas but would not be ruled by *Intombazanencane*.[2] But I was strong.

In time DRC merged with other Soweto organisations to form the Soweto Electricity Crisis. I was nominated to be Chair of the coalition. I doubted myself so I thought I'd get someone experienced and a male comrade became Chairperson and I became the Deputy.

Then, when time came for the AGM and for elections of new office bearers, he planted people in the AGM to make sure that I didn't become Chairperson.

As much as I was learning from him, I was also learning to question things. He made sure that I got isolated from the organisation that I had contributed to build. At the same time I was still a newlywed and I'd go to meetings and come back late. We were building SECC and APF at the same time. This posed a very big problem in my marriage. One day I came home and my husband was standing at the door and he said, "I think you need to choose." I told him I had chosen already.

Then I was isolated from SECC and APF. It was hurtful. But I told myself, "It's the struggle and it's bigger than me," so I put that aside and continued.

During the World Conference Against Racism in Durban, I gained a new profile and was in the media. I was travelling a lot and my profile was growing. My husband hit me when I came back from the conference.

The comrade had a group called the Socialist Group. I also got isolated from that. It was a very "male" space. When there were problems between me and my husband the same comrade would come to speak to me. One day he said, "Virginia, You should forgive him. Its okay. He has hit you for the first time, only once". But I decided to leave my husband eventually.

> *In every struggle, women are affected. Every struggle is a woman's struggle.*

" *We were building the SECC and APF at the same time. This posed a very big problem in my marriage. One day I came home and my husband was standing at the door and he said, 'I think you need to choose.' I told him I had chosen already.* "

There are situations where comrades say, "We fight for socialism." It is one of these big things they like to mouth, but they are so backward on women's rights. Even when I was in Cape Town, when I worked for the Alterative Information Development Centre (AIDC)[3], there would be men who would say "Virginia, you don't have a space to speak here. Go back to Joburg."

I eventually went back to Jozi to work for the Freedom of Expression Institute (FXI). It was a good space. It was a space where I regained my strength and confidence.

In all my organising experience, my saddest experience was to find out that even though many men are chauvinists, there are also women who do the same things to undermine other women. "Who does Virginia think she is? We're not going to attend a workshop organised by her," some women would say, just to show me.

There is no willingness to work with what Virginia comes up with because she's a woman. You find that it's men who are always at the forefront. This is the weakness of the organisations I've formed: they are good, but there isn't a strong effort to make sure that a woman's voice is heard. There is a policy of 50/50 (representation), but that's different from having women's voices heard and making sure that women who go into those structures are supported.

Women's socialisation is another challenge. When I was divorcing my husband, my mother said, "You can't be a woman if you act like that." Our mothers encourage us to be submissive. Patriarchy reproduces itself through the very people it's meant to subordinate: women.

Male comrades can kill the struggle by having affairs within organisations. Then the women fight with each other. We fight between ourselves. We fight over men. Men use sexuality to neutralise and demobilise us women.

"*In all my organising experience, my saddest experience was to find out that even though many men are chauvinists, there are also women who do the same things to undermine other women.*"

VICTORIES

I worked with women from the township and the youth. I feel that I assisted in developing other leaders. I feel proud when someone stands up and says, "I can speak today because of that woman."

I now work for the Norwegian People's Aid. We also do work on gender. We're in partnership with the Labour Party in Norway. There is a programme we run called "Women can do it". It teaches women how to speak in public, how to talk to the media and how to deal with men's domineering tactics. I'm enjoying my gender work now.

MOVING FORWARD

Not many women are strong, so some decide to leave the activist sphere because it is oppressive. It takes a lot of courage. There are too many sites of struggle. Sometimes you find yourself asking the question, "Do I really have to?"

Culture and socialisation play a big role in how women think and behave, amongst themselves and amongst men. Women will have to be their own liberators. We need to try to draw a line between culture and women's rights. It's difficult, but it needs to be done. If you are a woman who speaks up, you're not seen as a woman according to cultural terms.

We need a strong process of empowering and educating women. Sometimes you can be an intellectual but you don't know anything about organising. We need empowerment skills. Sometimes we say, "If a man isn't here, how will we run this meeting?"

In the movements, we need to support each other as women. We need to

> " *Patriarchy reproduces itself through the very people it's meant to subordinate: women.* "

create ways to learn from each other. It's not about learning from someone who has degrees; it is about learning from each other, women from working-class and poor communities. If you have that way of relating to women at all levels, they learn to respect you. We forget that if it wasn't for all these women none of us would be here.

Endnotes

1. University of Witwatersrand, Johannesburg.
2. A young girl.
3. http://www.aidc.org.za/.

"In the movements, we need to support each other as women. We need to create ways to learn from each other. It's not about learning from someone who has degrees; it is about learning from each other, women from working-class and poor communities."

Promise Mthembu

I was born and educated in KwaZulu-Natal. I have worked in the fields of HIV/AIDS and sexual and reproductive rights for 13 years at national, regional and international levels. I have a 17-year-old daughter.

> " *We felt we needed an organisation that is feminist and that can take women's issues further in more direct ways. As women we are usually the implementers, we work in organisations, we are the demonstrators, but we rarely formulate the demands or present the memoranda to officials.* "

I started to work on establishing an organisation in September 2008. It's called the Her Right's Initiative (Ilungelo Lakhe). It was formed to address the forced sterilisations of HIV-positive women. This is a huge issue and we need to challenge this through the courts. The organisation works on sexual and reproductive rights, particularly of women living with HIV. Issues of priority for the next few years are to address forced sterilisations of women living with HIV, cancer of the cervix as affects women living with HIV and gender-based violence as it is defined and experienced by women living with HIV.

I can say that setting up an organisation and accessing spaces is not easy. I suppose because we are women, have HIV, society thinks we have unusual issues – strategic interests – instead of teaching positive women to behave well and be good women.

Trying to set up an organisation has been really hard. I've belonged to many HIV/AIDS organisations in South Africa and globally. Trying to raise issues and get the issues into spaces like government, the Commonwealth Youth Programme and the South African Youth Commission has been a challenge.

As women living with HIV, we feel that treatment advocacy views us primarily as mothers. Programmes focusing on Preventing Mother to Child Transmission (PMTCT) ignore other aspects of what it means to be a woman. Yes, we are mothers, breadwinners, sisters, but we are also women in our own right. We want to take care of ourselves first but the treatment programming is centred around us being mothers and this means that we are unable to access treatment for issues that are key to us.

Cancer of the cervix is an example. There are no education programmes about this issue, and there are no treatment programmes for cancer of the cervix. If I have HIV, then I am immediately tested for TB. As a women, I should also be tested immediately for cancer of the cervix. HIV-positive women are ten times more likely to develop early cervical cancer, yet there is no testing. Lately there has been a lot of advocacy around the Human Papillomavirus (HPV) Vaccine.

This is good but it has its limitations because it assumes that women have sexually transmitted diseases and men are exempt. The vaccine will prevent women from being infected with the HP virus. But HIV-positive women are mostly exposed to HPV already and need treatment for abnormal pap smears. These are the two main issues we are hoping to address via our organisation.

I started the organisation in collaboration with other women living with HIV who are in leadership positions in other organisations. They are unable to adopt feminist approaches within their organisations because they are working within mainstream organisations with certain programmes and activities. We felt we needed an organisation that is feminist and that can take women's issues further in more direct ways. As women we are usually the implementers, we work in organisations, we are the demonstrators, but we rarely formulate the demands or present the memoranda to officials.

> " *The vision for women is to create and strengthen the political voice of women living with HIV in the country. Being a woman is a political identity and being HIV positive is a political identity. We need to use that.* "

VISION

Society must make it possible for teenagers to avoid pregnancy. Society must support teenage girls who fall pregnant. I was supported by feminists to apply for work overseas. Unless you have power or have access to people with power you don't have anything. I am a product of the feminist movement.

The vision for women is to create and strengthen the political voice of women

> *HIV/AIDS is a disease of poverty, patriarchy and social exclusion. It's a disease rooted in the division of labour in the global socio-economic and political system. You want a two-pronged approach. You want to give people treatment and you want to address the system: challenge capitalism so that is does not wreak havoc with people's lives in the way that it does.*

living with HIV in the country. Being a woman is a political identity and being HIV positive is a political identity. We need to use that. We want to identify strategic issues to say we are going to create spaces for ourselves to address these issues. Hence the three key issues: cancer of cervix, gender-based violence and forced sterilisations. We have identified these issues and are approaching them from a feminist political perspective. We are supporting HIV-positive women to claim their rights in society and in the courts.

HIV-positive women should be afforded the same rights as all women. My master's research topic is on cancer of the cervix and women living with HIV. I suggest that the lack of integration of cervical cancer preventation and treatment in HIV services is actually an extension of social exclusions faced by women living with HIV and all women. I am fascinated by the fact that women find it hard to make this issue and many others of high priority for themselves.

Cancer of the cervix, forced sterilisation and PMTCT all link to structural violence. When you get tested for HIV, you get medication to save your baby, but some women are given Depo Provera or get sterilised without their consent. In these cases, saving lives is taking away people's rights – this is not good.

ADVICE TO WOMEN WHO DO NOT HAVE ACCESS TO ANTIRETROVIRALS

HIV/AIDS is a disease of poverty, patriarchy and social exclusion. It's a disease rooted in the division of labour in the global socio-economic and political system. You want a two-pronged approach to address it. You want to give people treatment and you want to address the system: challenge capitalism so that is does not wreak havoc with people's lives in the way that it does. Women do a lot to subsidise patriarchy and capitalism. You want to come up with policies that are more developmental and social in orientation. I believe in social policy that is holistic and addresses gender, policies which incorporate social and economic needs because the two are two sides of one coin. Give a woman a grant and make sure she does not have to spend the grant on medical fees or school fees. Have a system that addresses the needs of people whether they have HIV or not, rather than adopting a minimalist approach. Make sure the treatment packages given to women are relevant and necessary. Think of a woman as a patient with particular needs relating to her sex. Women are people. They are social and political beings.

CONTEXT

Looking at my experience, I wrote my matric in 1994. I grew up in a culture of organising and mobilising against apartheid although I did not fully comprehend what I was doing. After 1994 there was a culture that you should work together as a unit, that we should stop challenging the government. But around 1998 and 1999 we could see that unless we challenge we are not going to get anywhere, or get anything. 1999 to 2000 was a traumatic year for me. I worked in government, for the South African Youth Commission, trying to understand and respond to HIV/AIDS from a youth perspective.

In 2000, suddenly according to our government, HIV did not cause AIDS. We did not have space to organise. We were failures because we had HIV. We became further marginalised and socially excluded. It was hard to talk about our issues for those of us who had come out about our status. We were public outcasts.

> " *Society embraces the women who are carers, not those who challenge things. They call them community builders, champions, because what they do fits the patriarchial model of a woman as a selfless carer who asks for nothing back.* "

The political context and nationalist AIDS discourses which characterised it in the last 12 years have a lot to do with where we are now. How could we advocate against forced sterilisation under the Mbeki era? Where living life "positively" was prescribed and yet was a lifestyle that was not attainable for many: how do you eat properly, get exercise, avoid stress, prevent and treat opportunistic infections timeously when the clinics expect you to only come when you are sick and so many people live in poverty?

It took the ANC government a long time to commit to PMTCT discourses; if it had not been stigmatised maybe the Treatment Action Campaign[1] (TAC) would not have identified PMTCT as its focus. This has turned out to be catastrophic for women. If you look at the PMTCT TAC logo, women are invisible; all it shows is the womb/stomach of the woman with a foetus in it.

The nationalist discourses under Mbeki's leadership advocated that people should die at home. When there is no treatment at the clinics and hospitals, what must people do? What must nurses do if not to send you home to die? This increased the power of patriarchal traditional healers and medicine, and shifted the burden of care to poor women in the form of home-based care programmes. In these programmes, women give care; they use their labour to care for the sick, the state gives them a stipend if they are lucky but most women don't even get that.

The role of multinational institutions in furthering the oppression of women must be pointed out. UN agencies, the World Bank and others were the first to advocate for home-based care programmes, knowing that in many contexts, it will be women who give care, while the state will not compensate or protect them from exposure to HIV and TB and other threats as they do their care work.

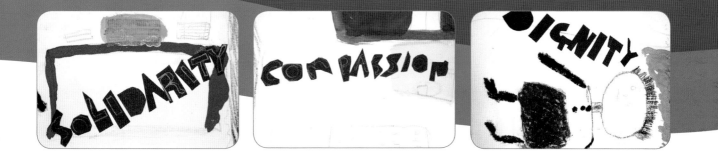

These institutions are part of the patriarchal machinery in the world. Patriarchy and capitalism support and reproduce each other.

Some of it has to do with the fact that after 1994 South Africa did not have a strong women's movement. Some women went into Parliament. We had commissions like the Human Rights Commission[2] and the Commission on Gender Equality.[3] But they have never said anything clear about women. This has a bearing on where we are now. We do not see many HIV-positive women leaders – women are carers.

Media tends to promote HIV-positive women who blame themselves for having HIV, not those who blame patriarchy or capitalism and the way society marginalises and excludes people. Society embraces the women who are carers, not those who challenge it. They call them community builders, champions, because what they do fits the patriarchal model of a woman as a selfless carer who asks for nothing back. This kind of volunteerism is a continuation of the patriarchal project which locks women in specific roles. It doesn't mean that what many women do is not good, but it's important that we be critical of the ways in which we continue to help patriarchy and capitalism reproduce themselves, even when it comes from our hearts.

What is important to women is where the next meal is going to come from. In women's daily lives, where is the time for rights or anything else? This makes organising on HIV difficult, even with the home-based care issue. It will take lots of feminist political education and organising on the ground to make women understand that in the end, we are contributing in our own oppression by continuing to believe the lies we are told about how we will get stipends and qualifications at some point if we volunteer as home-based carers without pay now. Yes, it is hard to watch our people struggle at home alone. We are bound to want to help. But HIV/AIDS and the way that our government and international community has responded has created other layers of exploitation of women and their labour.

VICTORIES

We documented stories of HIV-positive women. We worked with the Women's Legal Resources Centre and are preparing court papers.

Donors and some international organisations are approaching us and have asked us to speak to HIV-positive women in other Southern African communities. So there is regional recognition of the issues of forced sterilisation.

It's fulfilling to see HIV-positive women change and come into their own. I co-founded a programme called the Young Women's Dialogue Programme. This programme involved women from East and Southern Africa. Then we also did national programmes in South Africa, Namibia and Swaziland. These national workshops were held with HIV-positive women to talk about their issues. Statistics say young women are more vulnerable and more affected, but you do not see or hear from them.

It's been a long struggle. In 2002, Sisonke Msimang and I decided to apply for a satellite event at the AIDS Conference in Barcelona. It was approved but no-one came to the satellite. One young woman who was not HIV positive attended. We asked where the young women were, and from there began our organising in East and Southern Africa. It is fulfilling to see young women go through the programme and see their identities change. "I leave this place with a new identity, I am a now a young woman living with HIV," said one workshop participant. Young women graduated from our week-long programme on sexual rights, reproductive rights and rights to education about living with HIV. It's a structured programme lasting four days. On the last day policy makers are invited to interact with the young women. The policy makers came to the workshop and one women said we have sound evidence that HIV-positive women are being sterilised in this country and the Deputy Health Minister asked for the evidence and the cases were presented to them. One of these cases is currently being reviewed in a Namibian court.

CHALLENGES

It is difficult to get funding to do this work. Wherever you go donors think that you are duplicating work. Donors and the broader NGO community find it hard to understand the work. The donors pick and choose their favourites – the established organisations, the head boys and head girls. It's difficult for our organisations to have resources. It's difficult to get legal status, yet donors insist on it. When one key woman leader leaves or dies, the organisations tend to die as well. We are a "risky sector", but we also need to be supported and funded. It is difficult to mobilise the anger of HIV-positive women. Perhaps it's lack of space or power. Sometimes we get jobs in organisations and then we can't disturb the balance because we have vested interests and the agendas are controlled. There are not many spaces where women can sit together and talk about their issues. Safe spaces work. In mixed spaces men and women will talk about treatment and nutrition but in safe spaces women talk about their vaginas, sexual pleasure, warts, abortions, sterilisation, body

> *" Through my studies I learned that the issues are the same for women; we need to interact with women in housing, water, the informal economy and all other issues. Policies are not friendly to HIV-positive women, and they are not friendly to women generally. We need to reach out more across our divides. Everything is linked. "*

image and other critical issues that matter to us. The establishment of women's desks is quite counter-productive to women's causes.

MOVING FORWARD

As HIV-positive women, we need to work more with other formations, other women do not understand what our issues are. Sometimes we get locked in our issues and do not appreciate the struggles of other women, but it's all linked. Through my studies I learned that the issues are the same for women; we need to interact with women in housing, water, the informal economy and all other issues. Policies are not friendly to HIV-positive women, and they are not friendly to women generally. We need to reach out more across our divides. Everything is linked.

Endnotes

1. www.tac.org.za.
2. www.sahrc.org.za.
3. www.cge.org.za.

“*We had commissions like the Human Rights Commission and the Commission on Gender Equality. But they have never said anything clear about women.*”

Desiree Nolubabalo Higa

I am a lesbian activist and an artist, living, working
and organising in Khayelitsha, Cape Town.

I've been out since I was 18. I have a very good friend who was an activist, she was older than I was and she sensitised me to the lesbian movement and feminism. I wasn't that way inclined before I met her. I wasn't very active at the time; my energy was spent on my concern with teenage-hood and partying.

OUT AND ORGANISING

But from there I got involved in organising and it became a part of my life. I am a member of a group of women know as the Women Empowerment and Leadership Programme (WELP). It is a project that is coordinated by the Triangle Project.[1] As lesbian women, we get together, sit down and talk about the challenges we are facing in our different areas. Together we try to find ways of dealing with the challenges.

Now when someone calls me up and says, "Hey, there's a picket going on at such and such a place," I'm there.

The vision of WELP is to empower women, lesbians in particular, living in different parts of Cape Town, to build our own safe spaces and discuss, so we get to a point where we feel strong and deal with our own issues instead of going outside of our townships to seek help elsewhere. WELP gives us tools to do this for ourselves.

NO EASY BREAKS

This kind of work is critical at the moment. I've been thinking about it for a long time. I saw an advert in a gay and lesbian publication talking about a certain organisation where gay and lesbian business owners would get together, share ideas and network. When I thought about this, I thought wow; it's a really good idea: getting gay and lesbian people to sit down and actually do things for each other because we are in a

> *As lesbian women, we get together, sit down and talk about the challenges we are facing in our different areas. Together we try to find ways of dealing with the challenges.*

situation where it's every dog for himself and its difficult to be lesbian and out in South Africa, you don't get many breaks. That's why it's so important to have those people who are able to facilitate those types of connections and relationships to do so.

Our society is very patriarchal; it is constructed in specific ways. If you're not a man who is looking to find a woman, settle down and have children, you are not thought of as being worth much. This family model is like a type of status symbol. If you don't do this, or fit the mould, you are nothing and you don't deserve anything. People prevent you from getting anything that you are entitled to as a human being simply because of your sexual orientation. As gay and lesbian people we are not any less worthy, any less talented, any less intelligent.

We have laws and rights on paper but how they are being enforced, if at all, is the biggest problem. Our mind-sets have to change, they are locked in a frame that … it's incredibly difficult.

So for example, what is going on with one of our best female runners, Caster Semenya, is ridiculous. She's the best in her field, but people can't just appreciate that, they just have to bring her down somehow. You know these questions about her gender, why are they asking all these questions now? She's been running for many years. Why do they bring this up now?

The Caster Simenya issue is most definitely a violation – fuelled by the media who are not being helpful to get to the issue, they are just interested in selling newspapers. The issue is not about gender testing, whatever that is, it's about the system that says you have to look a certain way and be a certain way.

Caster is lucky in that she is a celebrity; she is maybe not as vulnerable as one would be if one was lesbian, unemployed, penniless living in a township, in that

> " *The vision of WELP is to empower women, lesbians in particular, living in different parts of Cape Town, to build our own safe spaces and discuss, so we get to a point where we feel strong and deal with our own issues instead of going outside of our townships to seek help elsewhere.* "

same situation. Positioned in this way you are very vulnerable. It is very easy to be killed for being a lesbian. People haven't moved on from the stereotypes that they had long before we actually got our freedom to be who we are. It's sad. But that's where it starts. It takes one person who says something about your difference, then everyone looks on and says you are right. This then propels people, other people join and join, and then it moves everyone into a mob mentality: "Let's get them, let's get them, let's get them," and that's when the violence occurs. People have to be careful what they say because anything can provoke violence.

CRITICAL ISSUES

Our WELP meetings have shown that drug abuse is a big issue, corrective rape is on the increase, and unemployment is rising. A lot of out lesbians of school-going age have parents who cut them off based on parental disapproval of the lifestyle their daughters have chosen. Being cut off means parents will not spend a cent on you. Denying someone an education is the worst thing you can do to someone. It means you've thrown the person out, locked all the doors and blocked that person's future. They can't get anywhere. This is happening as we speak.

In the Paarl WELP group a big problem is discrimination. There are a couple of members who are still in school and they are butch lesbians. They are discriminated against by teachers and peers. For example, whenever there is a school outing they are excluded from it under the guise that they are not adhering to the dress code: wearing dresses and skirts and for the outing that is a requirement. They are ostracised. The teachers start the whole thing, yet it's the teachers who are supposed to ensure fairness and equality. Teachers instigate other children to engage in this

> " *Our society is very patriarchal; it is constructed in specific ways. If you're not a man who is looking to find a woman, settle down and have children, you are not thought of as being worth much.* "

kind of discrimination and policing. What kind of society are they grooming?

As WELP we have community meetings, and every now and then members from all the communities come together in a workshop where we discuss and learn, for example issues of leadership.

But instead of getting better things are getting worse. South Africa is making a shift backwards. The moment you say anything about it you are public enemy number one. You have to be careful what you say. The anger is always there. The violence is always possible.

LANGUAGE TO TALK ABOUT SEXUALITY

Talking about sexuality is to talk about very private things. It is very difficult to talk about sex, no matter who you are. Perhaps it's only guys who feel that safe at all times to be talking about sex. But in our last workshop we had a nice lively discussion about sex and it was just lesbians and one gay guy. I think we've gotten to a place where we trust each other enough to feel safe to talk about those types of things with each other. There is a feeling of belonging which means that we can talk about everything and anything. Trust is important and a safe space is important. We have community meetings at each others' houses and the joking becomes bawdy at times and it's comfortable, it's nice, knowing that we feel absolutely safe.

UNSAFE SPACES

I have a friend who is about 19. We were in the train and we were chatting. A train is a very public space and when we walked into the carriage we got glances. There were around six or seven guys near us, two of whom were very interested in our conversation and I was scared because she was being very candid talking about sex at the time.

They would invite themselves into the conversation by saying something meant to make us angry. This is where it starts. It is very easy to move from there to violence. I didn't say anything and I didn't try and stop the conversation. We were lucky. My friend hasn't really seen the hurtful side of being gay: when you get beaten up, raped – those things haven't happened to her and I wouldn't wish them to happen to her, ever. But that's how it starts, an innocent comment and it triggers violence.

I can think of two incidents of violence against lesbians that were instigated by women. I don't understand how it makes sense. Just because you are in a woman's body doesn't mean you have politics that's not seen as patriarchal.

EMOTION FUELLING ACTION

There are many things that are hurtful. You have to get to a point where you take the bad energy and use it for something good, make sure that everything you do, you do thoroughly. Whatever you have to organise you throw the energy of what has happened, of how bad you feel, into doing something about it. If you go into something not feeling it, you shouldn't be there. After all this is about our lives, my life and your life, and if you're not passionate about it, what does that say about how you see your life?

THINGS ARE GOING TO CHANGE

Getting recognition from people is really important for me in this struggle. I don't mean recognition as in, "Oh, you're so wonderful," but having people realise, "She is a lesbian, she's been through so much and she's still identifying publicly as a

> *If you don't ... fit the mould you are nothing and ... people prevent you from getting anything that you are entitled to as a human being simply because of your sexual orientation.*

lesbian. Nothing has changed." I like to feel that people who are judgmental and prejudiced actually walk off feeling defeated.

I love knowing that it won't always be like this. That's the thing about life, it's always changing. We are in the struggle and we'll be there for a long time, but in time things will change.

CHALLENGES

The challenges faced on a daily basis could be something as simple as getting a seat in the bus and not being bothered by anyone until you have to get off where you get off. Without anyone staring, passing remarks, trying to goad you into a war of words, when all you're trying to do is get home.

Another challenge is to be heard. Often we are given platforms to speak, but being heard is different. Making people listen is a huge challenge.

It's easy to have a defeatist attitude – as lesbians you feel no one will listen to you – but getting to a point where you say, "I know who I am, I know what I'm worth," and saying what you have to say without apologies, is a victory. The way the other person reacts is entirely up to them. It's their problem.

" As gay and lesbian people we are not any less worthy, any less talented, any less intelligent. "

MOVING FORWARD

This is a cliché but it does make sense to me. It doesn't matter how many times you fall down, it's actually how many times you get up that matters. As human beings we get depressed and despondent, but willing yourself into action and doing something that makes the day worthwhile for you is what is important to me.

Endnote

1. www.triangle.org.za.

A LIFE OF NO CONSEQUENCE

Born of the mothersoil,

destined for greatness

An acorn in which an oak was embedded

greedy eyes watched while evil laboured their hearts

Her sin, her blasphemy –

Her sex – her skill

Her knowledge of self

Slowly, they trimmed her branches

"This was necessary they said", as she was growing wild!

She watched in silence

As her branches fell

Shadows crept into her soul

Her leaves grew back, as leaves often do.

She watched herself in amazement and awe.

Wild but free, her spirit soared

She saw them approaching,

most with scissors in hand.

No more! she shouted.

No more will you trim and prune me!

Some cheered, but most left in disgust.

> *Talking about sexuality is to talk about very private things. It is very difficult to talk about sex, no matter who you are.*

Finally at peace to go about her business, she grew.

They watched!

Her stem grew thicker, her leaves flourished,

and still they watched

Most in horror, some in amazement.

Until one dark night,

most came with axes and chopped her down,

she fell in silence

and some forgot!

" I love knowing that it won't always be like this. That's the thing about life, its always changing. We are in the struggle and we'll be there for a long time, but in time things will change. "

Zimbabwe Solidarity Action: Women speak out, 13th November 2008, Centre of the Book, Cape Town..

Conclusion: Already Bold, We Must Be Even Bolder[1]

The 19 reflections on struggle and resistance which constitute this book are a fraction of the large body of evidence that shows just as we have been oppressed, exploited and dehumanised through time, we continue to dream, resist and build alternatives for our lives and our world. In listening to the individual stories and the collective voice, we realised that an understanding of the working of patriarchy was vital in order to make sense of our experiences. This required identifying the common threads from our individual chapters, pulling them out in order to weave them together again to craft an analysis that is more than the sum of its individual parts. In doing this we realised that there isn't always a language to explain how it is that we come to be schooled in the art of patriarchy. Sometimes we have to redefine words or even make words up to name and speak to our realities. We also realised that being embedded within an oppressive system does not take away from our agency. What we do has an effect on the system in small and sometimes big ways. We have in different ways journeyed to boldness in confronting patriarchy; these journeys from the personal to the political are in fact the substance of our activism. Ultimately, the stories are signatures for hundreds and millions of women in the world, organising in different ways to challenge patriarchy and its varied manifestations which threaten to take everything we have: our dignity, our humanity, our freedom.

COLLECTIVE ANALYSIS FOR COLLECTIVE ACTION FOR CHANGE: EDUCATION IN THE SCHOOL OF PATRIARCHY

Patriarchy is the single most life-threatening social disease assaulting every aspect of our lives. Yet most people in our societies and communities do not use the word "patriarchy" in everyday life. They never think about patriarchy: what it means, how it is created and sustained. The word "patriarchy" is not a part of most people's "normal" everyday thought or speech. Some people who have heard the word usually associate it with women's liberation, with feminism, with imperialism, an illogical radicalism, and therefore it is dismissed as irrelevant to their own experiences.

Patriarchy is a political–social system that insists that males are inherently dominating, superior to everything. Everyone different from the constructed and sanctioned or approved understanding of masculinity is deemed weak, and is relevant only so far as they support and prop up men. It is a system where males are endowed with the right to rule and to maintain that dominance through various forms of violence. At its core, patriarchy is a set of institutions, symbols and ideas that make up a culture and which is embodied by everything. Patriarchal culture includes ideas about the nature of things, including the state, governance, the family, religion, the media, the law, education … life. It's about how social life is and how it's supposed to be; about what's expected of people and about how they feel. It's about standards of femininity and masculinity – it's about defining women and men as opposites, assuming they complete and "fit" together, about the "naturalness" of male aggression, competition, and dominance and of female caring, child minding, cooperation, and subordination. It's about the valuing of a particular constructed masculinity and heteronormativity and devaluing a

> " *Patriarchy is the single most life-threatening social disease assaulting every aspect of our lives. Yet most people in our societies and communities do not use the word 'patriarchy' in everyday life. They never think about patriarchy.* "

particular and constructed femininity and femaleness. To live in a patriarchal culture is to learn what's expected of us as men and women, the rules that regulate punishment and reward based on how we behave and appear.

All the women in this volume have been standing in their communities, at podiums, in fora, talking about and challenging patriarchy. It is a word we choose to use daily, and men who hear us use it often ask what we mean by it. These interactions are rarely supportive; they are sometimes loudly, and sometimes silently, hostile. Often they are "neutral" where feminism is understood to be a variety of Marxism for girls, or associated with women joining men in the ranks as equals without questioning accountability for sexist roles, actions or the disruption of male privilege. Many women in this volume use the phrase "capitalist patriarchy" or "imperialist, capitalist patriarchy" to describe the systems that are the foundation of a politics that informs and infuses our lives, locally, nationally, regionally and globally. This is indicative of African women's histories with regards to experience of colonial domination and class hierarchies, which has a direct link to race and our understanding of the ongoing dispossession of the majority. From a young age the system that we come to know most intimately and which is the least politicised is in fact the system of patriarchy. Even if we never know the word, patriarchal gender roles are assigned to us as children and we are given continual guidance about the ways we can best fulfil these roles.

Our sense of gender roles is learnt at a very young age, usually from our parents or caregivers. As Sipho noted in her interview, "my political consciousness and feminist education did not begin in an organisation. It began in my home." As daughters we are taught that our role is to serve, to be weak, to be free from the

All the women in this volume have been standing in their communities, at podiums, in forums, talking about and challenging patriarchy. It is a word we choose to use daily, and men who hear us use it often ask what we mean by it.

burden of thinking, to nurture others. We are taught it is "not proper" for a female to be violent. As sons we are taught our role is: to be served; to provide; to be strong; to think and act, not to express emotion. These roles are sanctioned by the church decrees that women were created from man and must forever be subservient, and reinforced by every institution we encounter.

Many of us can relate to Virginia's experience: "At the time I became an organiser, I was a newlywed. I was young. There were older people who had been in the struggle – in the ANC or the PAC – who considered themselves more experienced than me. They thought I had good ideas but would not be ruled by *Intombazanencane*."[2] We are taught that these hierarchies of age and gender are "normal" ways to organise life. When we point this out, we are accused of being extreme and exaggerating. When we try and do things differently, we bump into the power of the "norms" which our children are fed in school, on television, through popular music, adverts, everywhere.

In cases when we do "transgress", be it little boys playing with Barbie dolls or little girls wanting to herd cattle, we get physically and emotionally beaten so that we acknowledge that we understand what we have done. The rage and violence metered out to transgressors captures everyone's attention. Sometimes it is explained by women close to us: "I tried to warn you. You need to accept that you can't do that." In the service of patriarchy some women work to reinforce and restore the "natural social order". The beating, literal or figurative, serves as a reminder to everyone and anyone who may be watching/remembering, that if we do not obey the rules, we will be punished, punished even unto death. This is the way we were experientially schooled in the art of patriarchy.

"In our families," says Mamy, it is the "mother-in-law who says you mustn't tell anyone if your husband fights with you or beats you … she tells us not to go to the police because he will divorce us." Virginia further explains: "When I was divorcing my husband, my mother said: 'You can't be a woman if you act like that'. Our mothers encourage us to be submissive. Patriarchy reproduces itself through the very people it's meant to subordinate: women." It's no wonder that many women do not want to be confrontational. That so many of us fear the repercussions we will face if we threaten patriarchy. There is nothing unique or even exceptional about this. Listen to the voices of women and men and you will hear different versions with the same underlying theme: the use of violence to reinforce our indoctrination and acceptance of patriarchy.

UNLEARNING THE LEARNING

Since we're stuck in a model of social life that to a large extent views everything as beginning and ending with individuals, we have trouble understanding how systems like patriarchy work apart from individual behaviour and attitudes. Patriarchy's defining elements are its male-dominated, male-identified, and male-centred character,[3] but this is just the beginning. These are all characteristics that are cleverly hidden in plain sight and it takes a certain eye to see and realise the depths to which these characteristics intrude upon our lives.

Our society is male dominated in the sense that we equate powerful positions with maleness and expect, and at times insist, on seeing men in governmental or societal positions where power is wielded. We expect our president to be male. We expect our doctors, our lawyers, our Supreme Court judges, heads of households, even our spiritual officials, all to be male and we expect everyone in these positions,

> *Our society is male dominated in the sense that we equate powerful positions with maleness and expect, and at times insist, on seeing men in governmental or societal positions where power is wielded.*

including women, to act like men. We are surrounded by extended families, state institutions, and cultural and religious practices that dictate that the place for women is under men in a male dominated system. The male heads negotiate *lobola*; a father gives his daughter away at a wedding to symbolise the family acceptance that she now belongs to her husband, whose surname she takes on. Women are valued as mothers, and neglected at best and violated at worst when they reject these roles.

Promise explained what this has meant for women with HIV: "Treatment programming is centred on us being mothers and this means that we are unable to access treatment for issues that are key to us. Cancer of the cervix is an example. There are no education programmes about this issue and there are no treatment programmes … if I have HIV, then I am immediately tested for TB. As a woman, I should also immediately be tested for cancer of the cervix. HIV-positive women are ten times more likely to develop early cervical cancer, yet there is no testing." Focusing on women only as mothers "has turned out to be catastrophic for women", she said, because it creates resources only for women playing out one possible role – as reproducers.

Male dominance doesn't just create in us assumptions about family structures, gender roles, our worth as women and that people in power are always and should always be male; it creates a doubt in us that those who are not male can't handle the rigors and responsibilities associated with that power. Virginia described how this affected her early days of organising in the Soweto Electricity Crisis Committee: "I was nominated to be Chair of the coalition. I doubted myself so I thought I'd get someone more experienced, and Trevor Ngwane became the Chairperson and

I became the Deputy." Society dictates that there must be a head of household and from a young age boys get practice speaking and leading, which feeds the argument that they are "truly" more qualified for the position. In this way, women get more practice taking care of children, which feeds the argument that they are "truly" more qualified to remain at home and in the kitchen.

This self-fulfilling prophecy was described by Nosipho: "Most women are not given an opportunity to attend workshops because there is no translation and they don't understand English." Mamy also talked about this situation: "Usually men are the leaders, and they undermine women, saying she doesn't know how to speak English, or she doesn't know this or that, so you just shut your mouth and don't want to continue." For her this was not a issue separate from the lessons on how to behave as an obedient "wife" as enforced by her mother-in-law.

When women do transgress these boundaries, and become strong leaders, they are called crazy, labelled as lesbians or "home breakers". And when men transgress these boundaries and cook and clean and cry, they are insulted with words implying they are more female than male: "*moffie*", "jy is *'n poes*", "bitch". Mamy joked about how women learn to cross these boundaries: "As a leader I also want to use the big bombastic words that the comrades use. That way you can have the crowds cheer and roar with you. That is how it is done." We all laughed and remembered how many of the people called leaders, mostly male, were put in those positions on the basis of bombastic words, and how many times we ourselves were carried away with the power of their voices so we forgot to listen to what they were saying, to the words they choose to use as well as those they choose not to use. Throughout history, the militancy of struggles and their leaders is measured on the basis of

how loudly the leaders speak, how powerfully they deliver their speeches, how masculinist they sound. Squeaky voices just do not cut it.

Another joke circulates in some women's meetings. We clear the throat, then say: "Sorry comrades, I am busy preparing my shop steward's voice." Because, says Virginia: "If you are a woman who speaks up, you're not seen as a woman according to cultural terms." Then, you must proceed to speak and posture like a man. That way you capture the crowds. For a long time most shop stewards on the factory floor were men, and the male political culture got assimilated as the way to behave as a fit leader. Where, then, is the place for the woman, the gay man, the lesbian woman or the transgendered person, who has a high-pitched voice but has rock-solid ideas? The soft-spoken one whose truth is simply unquestionable?

The language of middle-class technicists and neoliberal policy makers achieves the same thing and in many of our organisations it is used to maintain the power and privilege of middle-class or working-class elites. This turns people's realities into dead and deadly technical concepts, statistics instead of material realities.

This influences not only the language and postures we adopt, but also the content of what we can and cannot say or suggest as ways of working for social change. The result is that many women in positions of power are barred from acting on women's agendas. As Anna commented: "You tend to have lots of women in the labour or social movements taking action, but few in the leadership, and even when they are in leadership it is often hard for them to act in women's interests. This is also reflected at the political level were there is a layer of women politicians and women within the state gender machinery who are entirely disconnected from black working-class women and their struggles."

When the occasional woman does "break through the glass ceiling" and attain powerful office, her ability is called into question. Not because she has any fewer qualifications for the job, but simply because she is not male and we have learned to confuse the position with the person in the position. So "the moment a woman stands up, women will be the first to criticise her", describes Mary. This "Pull Her Down (PHD) Syndrome" has been a painful experience for many of us. While men are equipped by society to use violence as a form of control and to punish threatening dissent, women are well trained in the art of social marginalisation and how to exclude and socially ostracise other women. Virginia explained: "In all my organising … my saddest experience was to find out that even though many men are chauvinists, there are also women who do the same things to undermine other women.'Who does Virginia think she is? We're not going to attend a workshop organised by her,' some women would say, just to show me. There is no willingness to work with what Virginia comes up with because she's a woman. You find that its men who are always at the forefront."

Male centeredness is an even more invisible characteristic of patriarchy in our society because we are so strongly heteronormatively male identified that we rarely notice it. Heteronormativity is a term to describe the marginalisation of non-heterosexual lifestyles and the view that heterosexuality (sexual behaviour with or attraction to people of the opposite sex) is the "normal" sexual orientation. Instances of heteronormativity may include the idea that people fall into two distinct and complementary categories: male and female; that sexual and marital relations are normal only when between people of different sexes; and that each sex has certain "natural" roles in life. Thus physical sex, gender identity and gender roles should in any given person align to all-male or all-female cultural norms.

Desiree: "Our society is very patriarchal – it is constructed in specific ways. If you're not a man who is looking to find a woman, settle down and have children, you are not thought of as being worth much. This family model feels like a type of status symbol. If you don't do this, or fit the mould, you are nothing and you don't deserve anything. People prevent you from getting anything that you are entitled to as a human being simply because of your sexual orientation." The same applies to straight women who do not have children.

Patriarchy is male identified and life in general is centred on heterosexual masculinities, what society identifies as "real men" and their stories. Everywhere we go and everything we do, we can be certain that we will see examples of men and what men are doing. Women are taught to groom their bodies and carry themselves in ways that support the system. Only certain hairstyles, body types, and attitudes are acceptable. As Promise argued: "Society embraces the women who are carers, not those who challenge it. They call them community builders, champions, because what they do fits the patriarchal model of a woman as self-less carer who asks for nothing back." That is why, she argued, you will never see HIV-positive women on TV "who blame patriarchy or capitalism and the way society marginalises and excludes people".

Similarly, Desiree described how heteronormativity affects gay schoolgirls who reject wearing dresses. "They are butch lesbians. They are discriminated against by teachers and peers. For example, whenever there is a school outing they are excluded from that under the guise that they are not adhering to the dress code: wearing dresses and skirts and for the outing that is a requirement. They are ostracised." From emotional abuse to physical and socio-economic punishment we have experienced the range of possible outcomes of dressing or behaving in ways that disappoint the men in our day-to-day lives or the male dominated system in general. The consequences for both gay and straight women who take their own looks and dress into their own hands are lethal, as the examples given by Nosipho and Mamy about the stripping and beating of a woman wearing a miniskirt at the Joburg taxi rank show.

Patriarchy is obsessed with control. Many men, says Gladys "feel they need to be on top. They are betrayed if a woman is a leader in the community." Patriarchy requires male dominance by any means necessary; hence it supports, promotes, and condones sexist violence. We hear the most about sexist violence in public discourses about rape and abuse by domestic partners, in which the authority figure is deemed ruler over those without power and given the right to maintain that rule through practices of subjugation, subordination and submission.

Women in this volume have had axes taken to their faces by their partners, been beaten, abandoned, raped, and have survived child abuse. Sipho described a typical scenario of a gathering of women activists: "You are in a room with a rowdy group of singing women and then you start talking about your lives. Story after story reveals that in different ways, the women have been raped or violated in some way by a man, and in some cases, carry the childhood wounds of a mother who used her child as an outlet for the pain of her own violation by the system of patriarchy or racism." This happens to straight and gay women alike; the roots are the same.

Desiree explained how "it is very easy to be killed for being a lesbian. People haven't moved on from the stereotypes that they had long before we actually got our freedom to be who we are. It's sad. But that's where it starts. It takes one person

Patriarchy requires male dominance by any means necessary; hence it supports and condones sexist violence. We hear the most about sexist violence in public discourses about rape and abuse by domestic partners, where the authority figure is given the right to maintain his rule through practices of subjugation, subordination, and submission.

One in Nine Campaign action on the 4th memorial of the Zuma judgement, 11th May 2010.

who says something about your difference, then everyone looks on and says you are right. This then propels people, other people join and join, and then it propels everyone into a mob mentality: 'Let's get them, let's get them, let's get them', and that's where the violence occurs. People have to careful what they say because anything can provoke violence."

Homophobia is a part of sexism that makes life harder for both gay and straight women alike because of the rules it sets which justify using violence to "keep us in our places." Violence is always lurking just under the surface, ready to be used in the flash of an instant. For example, Desiree and her friend "were in the train … chatting. A train is a very public space and when we walked into the carriage we got glances. There were around six to seven guys near us, two of whom were very interested in our conversation and I was scared because … they would invite themselves into the conversation by saying something meant to make us angry. This is where it starts. It is very easy to move from there to violence … that's how it starts, an innocent comment and it triggers violence."

These power dynamics come with a whole set of rules to control sexuality. Liberating discourses on sexuality, pleasure and desire for women are deliberately repressed because sexual pleasure and eroticism have political implications. This has led to a conflation of sexuality and reproduction within a context that demands this and, where necessary, annihilates any violation of this "norm". It is considered "normal" for men to have more than one partner, to use violence to assert ownership over a woman, and unacceptable for women to do the same. When men are raped in situations of war, they are told they are now women. When casual workers are underpaid it is called a feminisation of labour. In each

> *Liberating discourses on sexuality, pleasure and desire for women are deliberately repressed because sexual pleasure and eroticism have political implications. This has led to a conflation of sexuality and reproduction within a context that demands this and, where necessary, annihilates any violation of this 'norm'.*

of these scenarios oppression and violence is justified by the deeply entrenched assumption that masculinity is defined as superior to femininity.

This is what justifies the devaluing of women's work in the home and the lowering of both women and men's wages in paid employment. Feminisation of labour, argued Shereen, means that: "The reproductive work performed by women in the household has been extended by outsourcing into the public sphere." Outsourcing is "a small part of a larger structural system which oppresses workers." In the home women continue to spend hundreds of hours carrying water, cooking, cleaning – and they are praised for this.

The South African state, for example, encourages people dying of AIDS to do so at home. Promise spoke about how the promotion of home-based care programmes where "women give care; they use their labour to care for the sick, but the state only gives them a stipend if they are lucky and most women don't even get that. The role of multinational institutions in furthering the oppression of women must be pointed out. UN agencies, the World Bank and others were the first to advocate for home-based care programmes, knowing that in many contexts, it will be women who give care, while the state will not compensate or protect them from expose to HIV and TB and other threats as they do their care work. These institutions are part of the patriarchal machinery in the world. Patriarchy and capitalism support and reproduce each other… This kind of volunteerism is a continuation of the patriarchal project which locks women in specific roles. It doesn't mean that what many women do is not good, but it's important that we be critical of the ways in which we continue to help patriarchy and capitalism reproduce themselves, even when it comes from our hearts."

Similarly, Nosipho described "All this volunteering, it's gendered that women do incredible work, but for free. We must recognise what we do as important and deserving of remuneration. We must see it as work." Patriarchy is a form of divide and rule. This set up is reproduced in our homes and in our work places: "the experience of a worker in one company is the same as a worker working in another company on another part of UCT's campus. The fact that they are kept apart from each other by the system only serves the purposes of the system," argued Shereen. Thus individual women are expected to take care of their own problems – childcare, health, labour exploitation, education, are not collectivised or prioritised at the state level.

Women then depend on other women's labour, younger women, daughters-in-law, domestic workers, women are set up to compete with each other and depend on controlling each other, to survive. The behaviour of other women plays a powerful role in reinforcing the decisions and positions we occupy. When we transgress these roles, our actions are felt as a threat to the entire system. This explains how women can instigate violence against lesbians, and why our mothers and our male comrades will not support our leadership, or why they tell us to stay in an abusive relationship as described in many stories in this book.

FEMINIST STRUGGLES WITHIN A PATRIARCHAL SOCIETY

Does all of this mean that our participation in the system has no effect on the system itself? Certainly not. There are implications for understanding patriarchy thus: although many people experience patriarchy as existing externally to them, we participate in it; we are of it and it is of us. Like capitalism, patriarchy isn't static, it's

an ongoing process that's continuously shaped and reshaped, re-inventing itself in order to maintain its currency and power. It takes a different tone in the home, the extended family, workplace, movements, circles of friends, places of entertainment, political debates in the newspapers – but at its heart, it is one system based on the idea that men are superior to women. Though we may not be able to change the core of patriarchy in one fell swoop, every choice we make has an effect in the system. And we all participate in the system, whether we realise it or not.

Most men unwittingly participate in the perpetuation of patriarchy because every man benefits from the system. He is granted power and privileges over women, whether he is individually powerful or not. These are powers and privileges that, were he to be completely aware of them, he would likely not choose to give up voluntarily. But power and privilege are not the only things that cause us to participate, however tacitly, in the perpetuation of patriarchy. Men especially, perpetuate patriarchy through paths of least resistance as well. After all, it is far easier to go with the flow than it is to try and swim against the current that is patriarchy.

A slight digression here: there are men who are committed to social change and progressive agendas. They have a responsibility to come to terms with the privilege that is associated with their assumed position under patriarchy, a process that is most certainly not easy. It requires a great deal of unlearning, questioning, and internal struggle. When you spend your entire life conditioned into a socialised masculinity, it becomes difficult to break from that mould. This is particularly true in a culture that threatens men who don't conform to heterosexist standards. Ultimately, feminism isn't just about women. It is about the ways in which we are all implicated by power structures, norms and unrealistic expectations. There are men who believe that they can be active members in the feminist struggle, rather than passive consumers. There is no excuse to scapegoat responsibility for the oppressive socio-political structure that we live under. These men support feminist principles; are committed to doing the necessary self-work in order to reject old notions of masculinity. They oppose all forms of misogynist behaviour and sexist attitude; believe in a woman's reproductive freedom and right to control her own body; understand the need for men to participate in feminist struggle and help end 2,000 years of men's patriarchy; pledge to support women in every possible way they can, including sharing responsibilities around the house and in parenting. They do this for women's emancipation, for the benefit of women, men and all humanity.

For women under patriarchy, however, it is a lose/lose proposition. Following the path of least resistance merely prevents further hardships or disadvantages, it doesn't actually protect a woman from hardship or disadvantage in the first place. Each and every day, women participate in patriarchy in a way that perpetuates the oppression experienced by all women. It is in the small, unnoticed things that we do every day. When it comes to participating in patriarchy in these ways, it becomes very difficult for women to make choices to take the path of greater resistance because, at that point, women are bucking not only under patriarchy, but major societal gender norms as well.

Promise put it this way: "Women do a lot to subsidise patriarchy and capitalism … It will take lots of feminist political education and organising on the ground to make women understand that in the end, we are contributing to our own oppression by continuing to believe the lies we are told about how we will get stipends and qualifications at some point if we volunteer as home-based carers

> *Ultimately, feminism isn't just about women. It is about the ways in which we are all implicated by power structures, norms and unrealistic expectations. There are men who believe that they can be active members in the feminist struggle, rather than passive consumers. There is no excuse to scapegoat responsibility for the oppressive socio-political structure that we live under.*

without pay now. Yes, it is hard to watch our people struggle at home alone. We are bound to want to help. But HIV/AIDS and the way that our government and international community has largely responded has created other layers of exploitation of women and their labour."

So where do we go from here? How do we unravel these knots? A great majority of individuals enforce an unspoken rule in the culture as a whole that demands we keep the secrets of patriarchy, thereby protecting it. This rule of silence is upheld when the culture refuses everyone easy access even to the word "patriarchy". This silence promotes denial and the normalisation of our lives and circumstances that are actually quite abnormal.

How can we organise to challenge and change a system that cannot be named? We fear challenging patriarchy even as we lack overt awareness that we are fearful, so deeply embedded in our collective unconscious are the rules of patriarchy. If we were to go door-to-door asking if we should end male violence against women, most people would give their unequivocal support. Then if you told them we can only stop male violence against women by ending male domination, by eradicating patriarchy, people would hesitate, change their position. Similarly, in our movements we are encouraged when we point out how neoliberalism is a war against women, but when we take the next step in demanding that our organisations take account of the gendered power dynamics and make changes that would take power away from men and male ways of doing things, we are personally attacked, our spaces are shut down, and we are often pushed out completely.

This belief seems ironic, given that patriarchal methods of organising people and nations, especially the insistence on violence as a means of social control,

> *Men especially are resistant to the deconstruction of patriarchy. After all, the end of patriarchy, means the end of male privilege.*

have actually led to the slaughter of millions of people on the planet. Until we can collectively acknowledge the damage patriarchy causes and the suffering it creates, nothing is going to change.

Men especially are resistant to the deconstruction of patriarchy. After all, the end of patriarchy means the end of male privilege. It means losing control over others and control over situations. It is easy to see how this would be distasteful to men who fear they have little to gain and a lot to lose from change. What men don't realise, however, is that they are already oppressed. Certainly, being male in our society has its privileges, but there is a price for those privileges. Men cannot be sensitive and still be masculine. They cannot be unemployed, or stay-at-home dads and still be fatherly or manly. They cannot show any sort of weakness or vulnerability without their manhood being called into question. And though it is not nearly the same sort of oppression that women experience, it is oppression nonetheless. If patriarchy were truly rewarding to men, the violence and addiction that is so all-pervasive would not exist. If men are to reclaim the essential goodness of male being, if they are to regain the space of openheartedness and emotional expressiveness that is the foundation of well-being, we must envision alternatives to patriarchal masculinity. We must all change. It is our hope that unravelling the knot of patriarchy will set us all free.

JOURNEYS TO BOLDNESS

Ntombolundi writes in her chapter: "My dream is to be bold and to oversee what is happening to my local municipality because the ward councillors are deployed by the community to represent us in the government." Like thousands of South

How can we organise to challenge and change a system that cannot be named? We fear challenging patriarchy even as we lack overt awareness that we are fearful, so deeply embedded in our collective unconscious are the rules of patriarchy.

Africans, she is determined to exercise greater agency in determining the context and conditions of her life and that of her community. She is already bold.

The 19 authors of this book share this determination to confront power. The journey to this realisation may be different for each person, but what is the same is that it is a discovery borne out of experiences of capitalist patriarchy. After starting monthly meetings in her sitting room with homeless backyard shackdwellers Lorraine saw how "it was mostly women … who had been on the waiting list for years, women who had jobs but didn't have enough money for bread after paying rent, women who survived off grants, women who were oppressed because of the system of patriarchy." She observes how "The system works against us. We have to struggle." Lorraine's conclusions that collective, politicised, feminist struggle was the only option echoes many of the journeys to confrontation shared in this collection.

Refugee women, said Mary Tal "were weary about some man somewhere always representing us and telling the world how we feel and what our needs are. We realised it was time we started speaking for ourselves, demanding our rights and letting the world know that we were tired of handouts." Dora described these shifts for herself: "When I first came to South Africa … I still had this feeling of 'I am a woman, I must not go to that limit.' When I heard other women speaking out and claiming their rights, then I felt empowered and can stand anywhere to talk about the Ogoni struggle and immediately connect it to the particular condition of women. I have come to the point that I would not give my own right to a man just because the person is a man, to rob me of my own right to speak."

At the workshop Gladys told the group about her journey thus far: "Patriarchy has brainwashed us. It tells us a man is a man … that he owns me. In the past I

> *The 19 authors of this book share this determination to confront power. The journey to this realisation may be different for each person, but what is the same is that it is a discovery borne out of experiences of capitalist patriarchy.*

couldn't do anything without asking my husband. Even if I want to go to the toilet! I finally said, "I can't go on like this." On some things I was failing to challenge this man. But now I'm proud because … we understand each other. He knows what I want, but before I was not like that I was 'Yebo, Baba, yebo, Baba,' and he would dictate things to me." Her resolve to take the risks of challenging and changing the dynamics in her partnership formed the basis of her desire "to start … a women's organisation". To confront the abuse that comes with patriarchy and the painful steps it takes to overturn it. To say to those willing to listen, "Hey wake up. We have to do this and this. It's up to us."

Jean described the ways in which "simple washing becomes stressful because women do not have enough water to do it all … this makes more work for the women and it controls us … as a woman you have no time for leisure because you are constantly busy. You get weak and sick. Every chore, even using the toilet, becomes stressful, because the water is rationed and you have to watch the meter all the time." The stress caused by women's reproductive responsibilities day after day, in household after household, became the basis for action in Mitchell's Plain.

The details of Glady's journey are written across her body: "One day I changed my hairstyle and my husband told me he didn't want it. I was supposed to go to a workshop and when he took me to the taxi he told me 'You look artificial'. I was feeling very bad … I said to Nosipho, 'How do I look?' and she said 'No, you look fine'. I told him after this hairstyle, 'I am going to do another one which is more artificial'. I continued to change my hairstyles until he sees that I will do what I want … We do not own each other. He does not own me. I go where I want to go and we speak on phone and arrange…. Not to say I don't respect him. But he doesn't own me. After all of these things I feel I am now living now a good life. There is a woman who brings her child to my daycare centre. Her husband is abusing her. He is having different affairs with the neighbours … I started sitting down with this women and said 'Let's take this on. It is a good struggle.' Together we talk and find ways to deal with her husband. Everything comes in my mind and I say we must start organising a women's organisation to deal with this man."

The shared life stories reveal how we each individually and collectively came to the feminist notion that the personal is political, how this forms the bedrock for action. Wendy expressed how "It is important for us to work with more people in the farm community … build solidarity and break the divide between work and what is personal. Today I am a worker, tomorrow I am an occupier of land." When we divide life between public and private, we divide ourselves and our realities. These are divisions that suit patriarchy, which tells us to deal with our own problems as individuals. If we don't have work, or water, or childcare, it is our problem alone, rather than a social and political problem to be solved collectively by changing social and political structures to suit our needs as humans.

We experience the injustice of homelessness, statelessness, the lack of basic services, inadequacy, and we are immediately angry, we rage through tears of humiliation, frustration, horror, and pain at the mutilation of our lives under the system. But eventually we reach a place where our rage is that of refusal, that of an assertion and a testimony to what is wrong and what has to change. The things that anger us are not isolated phenomena, there is a connection between them, they are all part of a world that is "wrong" in some fundamental way. Yet everywhere we turn, our anger is met by soundproof walls. When we express our

❝*The shared life stories reveal how we each individually and collectively came to the feminist notion that the personal is political. How this forms the bedrock for action.*❞

anger and voice our discontent at what is "wrong" with our world, we are told that we are being unreasonable. People look at us and ask: "Why are you performing?" or they roll their eyes saying, "Here we go again, those women!" or they just put it down to pre-menstrual tension. In this way, for fear of being seen as overreacting, we normalise what is actually completely abnormal. We are robbed of the validity of our rage. The structure disarms us, even though none of the things which made us so angry to start with have disappeared.

This makes the simple act of women sitting together and talking about their lives and problems a political act: saying what we really believe about our lives instead of what we've always been socialised to say. Personal problems are political problems. There are no personal solutions at this time; there is only collective action for a collective solution.

We see this in Gladys' description of the fight against prepaid water meters in Orange Farm; she spoke about the gender dynamics of whose problem it is, of how women collectively decided to resist, and to name the problem as a political problem needing a political solution: "We are the ones who feel the pain. We can't just sit and ignore this. So we stood up as a Women's Consortium to fight for water … We started to raise our voices." In these sharings, women often gain a political understanding which years of activist experience in mixed gender struggles will never give: a raw gut understanding of everything; a space where all parts of each of us are welcome.

Our stories are seldom if ever ours alone. They may be ours in terms of their specificity but the bare bones of our oppression as women are indicative of millions of women's life experience. Our narratives of journeying to boldness are

> *Our stories are seldom if ever ours alone. They may be ours in terms of their specificity but the bare bones of our oppression as women are indicative of millions of women's life experience.*

never linear, always unfinished, imperfect, limited and partial, even though we each claim feminism, underneath each of our voices resides a teeth-gritting and often contradictory intersection of voices constituted by gender, race, class, ability, ethnicity, sexual orientation or ideology. In spite of all the risks of self-exposure and violence, we have found that when we do take steps towards unravelling the knots of patriarchy so interwoven into each of our lives, this allows us to be bolder. In journeying to boldness there are instances where we are sometimes powerful and at other times powerless depending on our contexts and the situations imposed upon us.

POWER AND POWERLESSNESS

The work of dismantling patriarchy requires an understanding, interrogation and a mapping of how power works in different contexts. Yet power is a difficult concept to describe. The word power is derived from the Latin word *potere*, which means to be able. This root meaning focuses on power as a general capacity: we all have the potential to shape our lives and the world around us. However, based on most women (and men's) experiences in our current socio-economic and political context, power has more to do with control, influence or authority over others: "power over", instead of "power with" or "power to". Traditionally, power is thought of in terms of "power-over". "Power with" emphasises inter-dependence and collective action among community members and/or constituencies as a way of shifting and expanding power for the good of the whole, rather than the benefit of the few. Creating more just and equitable power relations, based on "power with" not "power over", requires building and exercising collective power among diverse groups.

> *The work of dismantling patriarchy requires an understanding, interrogation and a mapping of how power works in different contexts. Yet power is a difficult concept to describe.*

Power has multiple sources. It plays a role in shaping most social relationships and in determining who gets to decide important social, economic political and environmental questions. Often we can see power at work in very direct and obvious ways. At the same time, power operates in less obvious and even hidden ways, through cultural norms, traditions, religious discourses, ideas and practices that perpetuate existing power relations and that discourage questions about, or challenges to, those power relations.

Status quo power relations are reinforced by the fact that most of us experience powerlessness as part of everyday life. For most women and historically oppressed groups, the experience of being shut out of decision-making processes gets internalised and understood as the "natural state" of things – again normalising the abnormal. Adrienne Rich is useful here, as she observes: "When those who have the power to name and to socially construct reality choose not to see you or hear you … when someone with the authority of a teacher, say, describes the world and you are not in it, there is a moment of disequilibrium, as if you looked in the mirror and saw nothing. It takes some strength of soul, and not just individual strength but collective understanding, to resist this void, this non-being, into which you are thrust, and to stand up, demanding to be seen and heard."[4]

OVERCOMING POWERLESSNESS

A woman's individual sense of powerlessness is reinforced by the experience of social isolation. Too often, people who are removed from political and economic decision-making have no spaces in which to come together, think and discuss and struggle together to articulate their grievances into a set of demands. Denied

"We spend a lot of time filling and emptying buckets"

> "A radical feminist movement builds on the actions and words contained on the pages of the book. Such a movement has to make continual, daily choices about its positioning and practice."

the democratic experiences from which political consciousness can develop, the powerless instead develop a culture of silence.

In spite of the historical imbalances of power in this country and increasingly global corporate power over decision-making, agenda setting and meaning, there is a rich history of resistance to be drawn upon. As the voices in this book continue to show, feminist activists working in diverse communities and workplaces are giving women a place to act together, reflect on their actions, engage in collective analysis, and challenge power with new ideas and experiences. When they are combined, critical thinking and political action can break through the culture of silence. In this way we are challenging the common, if unspoken, assumption about power in our society: that unequal power relations are part of the natural order of things, and are, therefore, inevitable and unchangeable.

In chapter after chapter we have examples of feminist activists who are trying to alter power relations by building power for those who are marginalised and who are shut out of the arenas where the decisions are made that affect their lives.

In chapter after chapter we have examples of feminist activists who are trying to alter power relations by building power for those who are marginalised and who are shut out of the arenas where the decisions are made that affect their lives. From food sovereignty campaigns, to access to ARVs, to land, to decent working conditions, to education and housing, to refugee, sex-worker, and gay and lesbian rights, the activists in this volume have exercised "power with" through organising collectives that challenge the way power is wielded to control our lives. As Gladys noted: "We succeeded in stopping the pre-paid meters because we did it as a collective."

The authors have shared stories of confronting power "out there" as well as within our homes and organisations. Virginia described how frustrating it is that "there isn't a strong effort to make sure that a woman's voice is heard. There is a policy of 50/50 (representation), but that's different from having women's voices heard and making sure that women who go into those structures are supported." Mamy recently "became national Chairperson of the APF, because women voted me in, even though I was contesting against a man. While the man is educated, knows about the organisations and the politics, as women we say that you must learn by doing. We cannot learn politics and how to handle the organisation without the chance to learn, so the women insisted on me." Nosipho also spoke about the significance of this fragile victory: "Through Remmoho we have put a woman in leadership at APF. Mamy is now the Chairperson. But we know that putting women in positions of power without proper support can expose them to backlash, all forms of violence and emotional abuse. This means that as an organisation we will have to focus all our energy on trying to deal with the backlash."

In doing this often difficult and dangerous work, we often get shattered by the backlash. We often neglect ourselves. Many activists in this volume have spoken about feelings of being overwhelmed, traumatised, burnt out. The sheer volume of daily abuses that we witness as activists and the pressure to try and effect meaningful change can leave us feeling drained, shattered and/or depressed. We deprioritise ourselves for everything and everyone around us. The health of body, mind and emotions is continuously affected by trauma, violence, diet, environment, daily news, and the challenges of life. The challenge is to build into our lives and lifestyles practices of well-being and care that become second nature and can be readily called upon whenever we are aware of traumatic stress, energy drain, depressed feelings or loss of centre. This together with the solidarity of other women keeps us strong.

> *The health of body, mind and emotions is continuously affected by trauma, violence, diet, environment, daily news, and the challenges of life. The challenge is to build into our lives and lifestyles practices of well-being and care that become second nature and can be readily called upon whenever we are aware of traumatic stress, energy drain, depressed feelings or loss of centre.*

We grow collectively from our gains; for example Sikhula Sonke is now over 4,000 strong and continues to refuse to divide the personal and political or back down on core principles on a union for casual farmworkers, even as the membership of male and permanent workers grows. Young black lesbians continue to insist on accessible forums in townships to support lesbian organising. Building Women's Activism and Remmoho are other examples of some of the tangible gains that have been made and that must be guarded.

When organising and campaigns lead to victories for our communities and constituencies, we experience a heightened sense of our collective power, which opens up new possibilities.

> *When organising and campaigns lead to victories for our communities and constituencies, we experience a heightened sense of our collective power, which opens up new possibilities.*

Endnotes

1. Developed and written by Koni Benson and Shereen Essof in consultation with contributing authors.
2. A young girl.
3. See Johnson, A. (1997) The Gender Knot: Unravelling Our Patriarchal Legacy, Philadelphia, PA, Temple University Press.
4. Adrienne Rich as quoted in Maher, F A and Thompson Tetrault, M K (1996) The Feminist Classroom, New York, Basic Books, p. 1.

Out of the Pages of This Volume[1]

We sit, at the end of this volume with a multiplicity of voices, conversations, experiences and analysis. If we are committed, as Davine put it, to taking "the last step to end patriarchy", what are the critical lessons that can be distilled from our deliberations and inform our actions into the future?

In moving beyond the pages of this volume, we offer this last chapter as a perspective rather than a prescription flowing out of the collective voice of this book. To ensure we can identify power and the sources of women's oppression at every turn we need to arm ourselves with critical questions, which can be used in varied contexts, rather than models, answers or rules.

1. FEMINISM IS MORE OF AN APPROACH THAN A ONCE-OFF DECLARATION

Where do we start? The absence of a cohesive women's movement in South Africa has driven many women to a range of sites to voice their concerns and seek political platforms: we work within non-governmental organisations, social movements, community alliances, unions, churches, national liberation movements, in postcolonial contexts, and in state machineries. Regionally and globally, women sometimes locate their activism in international NGOs, development arms of state structures, the United Nations, global movements and coalitions. Are these sites conducive for women to put our energy and focus our activism?

When we push against patriarchy, even within these spaces, we are met with hostility. We find that even organising cultures do not always strengthen women politically and gender equality remains on the backburner, where women are welcome only to the extent that they remember their place is not in leadership, and certainly not asserting that gender relations and norms be transformed within the movements or organisations themselves.

To get around or evade this challenge, women have formed women's desks or women's groups. We hear in several authors' reflections of the challenges with this approach. While this has provided some space for women to reflect on their particular circumstances and act in solidarity, these groups get completely worn out, tired, beleaguered as they remain dependent on movements and organisations and are subject to their dictates. For many women in this volume the need to always fight for the starting point and defend a women's agenda at every stage along the way in the spaces where they choose to engage their struggles has led to frustration, constant tension, a drain in energy and at its most extreme, lack of will to continue. Many women have left organisations, campaigns and movements for these very reasons.

Perhaps the more critical question, then, is not where we choose to work or locate our activism, but what we want to do. Our collective voice has articulated it as follows: in order to dismantle patriarchy and end oppression we need to confront power. In creating the space for this kind of feminist struggle our search for allies must begin by insisting that women's voices be centred and that power be confronted. Men are welcome to join in this struggle but they must share this starting point and understand its implications. As Shereen said: "I don't necessarily care about labels, I don't care whether Nomonde chooses to name herself as a gender practitioner or

Linda chooses to name herself as human rights activist … what I care about is the politics that underpins what we are going to do … If we are constantly fighting and defending our positions before we can start the actual work we don't get anywhere. Our energy goes in negotiating the agenda with others. If my starting point is dismantling patriarchy and all other oppressive systems … at the end of the day power is the thing that we are confronting." Do we share this common ground? For this is the minimum standard or bottom-line for engagement.

QUESTIONS

- How do we ensure that we question the power at play at every turn – within our organisations, homes, work, relationships?
- Is women's liberation central or secondary in our collective visions that inform our activism and the plans and policies we draw up?
- What are the criteria for working together? What are the minimum requirements?
- When and which organisations do we choose to engage with?
- When do we leave and forge new types or organisations versus staying to fight?
- How do we hold ourselves accountable?

2. WOMEN-ONLY SPACES AND FEMINIST POLITICAL EDUCATION

To this end then, chapter after chapter has pointed to the value of maintaining women-only spaces, which are informed by feminist principles, as being vital to taking this agenda forward and building collective power and action. Often we are dissuaded from carrying this out by reactions that say, "We have moved beyond women-only spaces and all that now … What about gender equality? What about the men?" In Virginia's words: "Comrades say 'we fight for socialism'… but they are so backward on women's rights." Women in this volume are saying "No" to these claims.

Although we don't like to think of it all the time, the constant backdrop of our lives is that women are oppressed under patriarchy. We are caged and pressured at every turn – in the street, in our workplaces, in the queue at the train station or supermarket, in our political groups, and even in our homes. Sometimes it is hard to recognise the hot water until you get out of it. What women have testified to is that the value of creating and experiencing women-only feminist spaces in which feminist political education can be undertaken in an unfettered way is essential to bring about social change to combat the male-centred and male-dominant culture so much of the world struggles with. From these spaces, too, we can set our own agendas to counter what Promise described as the ways in which women leaders are "unable to adopt feminist approaches within their organisations because they are working within the mainstream with the constraints of pre-designed programmes and activities".

It is in autonomous women's spaces that a woman's voice can be heard on her own terms, where a women-centred politics can be forged without being compromised by dominant patriarchal voices and values that often worm their way in, taking us backwards rather than forward.

Creating solidarities that speak to who and where we are, as well as the politics we seek, is crucial too, and this needs to be supported by grounded feminist political education that allows us to get some perspective on our reality and begin to see, and develop alternatives to, the social forces we are embedded in and become inured or so used to it in our day-to-day lives. Insisting that women are thinkers, and can create theories and analyse our own situations, is vitally important, yet threatening, because if we as women are thinking for ourselves, creating our own analysis, we will come up with our own ideas on what actions to take, which can undermine patriarchy. As Anna noted, the kind of education women receive in a feminist political education curriculum is a lot more threatening than "gender training" or the training of "women leaders". Nosipho boiled down feminist political education to the links between the most personal and widest political struggles, saying: "Sexuality is central to all this. Once you realise that 'I am the owner of my body' and that we don't have to apologise to our husbands, our in-laws, that we can do what we want, we will begin to win the battle."

And while there can be feminist spaces with men in attendance, there is something indescribable and indispensable about women-only space that cannot be achieved otherwise. Of course, let us not be naive: creating a real alternative to patriarchy, and not just an enclave, will have to rely on men's experience and contributions. There are men doing exactly this kind of work and it should be supported and respected. Analyses of men's experiences under patriarchy are crucial to the work of creating a better, non-patriarchal world. Men may benefit from discussing these things in men-only spaces at times, but ultimately, our strategy has to determine how we engage in mixed gender spaces, when, why and to what end.

QUESTIONS

- What does it take to do "education" differently? What is feminist or political about the education? What is different about feminist political education – its topics? Its methodologies?

- How can these be spaces of thinking and action? What is the link between the two?

- How and when do we (or what do we need to) feel equipped to broaden our spaces or to branch out into the community?

- How do we support women in mixed-gender spaces through feminist political education?

- How do we prepare collectively for engaging in mixed spaces?

- What can men do to unlearn patriarchy?

3. THE PERSONAL IS POLITICAL

In feminist terms, the "personal is political" refers to the theory that personal problems are political problems, which basically means that many of the personal problems women experience in their lives are not their fault, but are the result of systematic oppression. The theory that women are not to blame for their bad situations is crucial here because women have always been told that they are unhappy or faring badly in life because they are, for example, stupid, weak, mad, hysterical, having a period, pregnant, frigid, over-sexed, asking for it, or not working/trying hard enough. The personal is political proposes that women are in bad situations because they experience gendered oppression and massive structural inequalities. Feminist political education allows us to understand that our oppressive situations are not our own fault or "all in our head". Women-only spaces and the solidarities therein give us a lot more courage as well as a more solid, real foundation on which to fight for liberation.

This also means that the solution is a political one. It is not that we as individuals need to adjust to the environment around us that is making our lives difficult, but rather the environment– or social/political/economic set up– around us that must be challenged to meet our needs and solve our collective problems. Politics is about distribution of resources, and the political does not just take place in places of "official" politics. As Sipho observed, "We need to challenge the state but the state can't be our sole focus because we understand that the nature of the South African state is itself patriarchal and liberal and that as women citizens we must exercise our agency to create the society we want to live in as much as we must extract from the state what is due to people in terms of the people/state contract." It is equally important that we challenge what is considered "normal" according to patriarchy in all the institutions in which our lives are embedded – the family, the media, education, as well as cultural and religious institutions.

Coming to this understanding hinges on the creating of space for women to talk about daily life, because it is in daily life that the political resides and reproduces. From this realisation we can develop analysis, strategy and action. Our feminist education curriculum needs to be as concerned with what goes on within the home as well as in the activist/movement of the left and it has to constantly make those connections. As Nosipho mentioned, "If we only work in one block, like only raising consciousness, but don't challenge informal cultural rules, we will not be able to see the shifts." As she says, this is because "most women have two voices:

one for the public and one for the private space. She can be strong and articulate. But what she practices is different … We need to begin to see the shifts in the private spaces because it is of no value if we are powerful in public spaces but can't change or interrogate informal and formal rules."

QUESTIONS

- How does patriarchy reproduce itself in each sphere of our lives?
- We need to be constantly vigilant to get an ongoing sense of the answers to the following questsions. How is patriarchy working to individualise, divide and dictate? What counts as political and why.
- What new avenues for oppression are being created as our socio-economic, political and technological contexts evolve?
- How can we formulate our personal problems into collective demands?
- What strategies can be used to carefully protect the gains won?

4.   FEMINIST COLLECTIVES AND THEIR PRACTICE

Meaningful social change does not come about by individuals working alone. Change comes through the organisation of people in a setting of mutual cooperation.

Building feminist collectives for change requires new kinds of situated solidarity that question power dynamics and imagine new ways of being. These would include: developing a culture of work that allows us to make decisions in an egalitarian environment; fair sharing of workloads and types of work; valuing cooperation over competition; working against sexism, racism, heterosexism, ageism, and classism; working by consensus, in ways that mean we put our minds together and work out decisions that contain the input of everyone because hierarchy and authoritarianism characterise patriarchy; working collectively with each person exercising her own authority, which requires high levels of trust, responsibility and accountability towards each other and towards the success of the project or action at hand; the joy, strength and inspiration to become, create and speak out; and the acceptance of women's bodies in all shapes, ages, sizes, and abilities.

In order for the collective to work through the challenges of this time and to envision and practice effective resistance we need to be able to "read" the new and rapidly changing geographies of power. The maps we need are inevitably collective projects, informed by the experiences, practices and knowledges generated by various struggles and waged from many locations. Often these struggles are informed by and led by middle-class women. But grounding our work in the politics of location in the Southern African context insists that we start with the situated position of the majority who are oppressed and this means centring the experiences of poor, working-class black women. Not only must we begin there, but we must also simultaneously map out how these conditions stand in relation to other women who may be positioned differently within a feminist collective in terms of power and inequality. We need to be constantly interrogating and monitoring our differences in terms of power differentials. Such a starting point can provide us with grounds for radical democratic practice. In these kinds of politicised spaces we are many, different, each with her story. The coming together and the alliance is neither natural nor a priori, given, but rather a continuous and conscious process of recognition and communication into which we launch ourselves again and again, committed to a strategy of uniting ourselves and overthrowing patriarchy.

QUESTIONS

- What are our differences and how do we speak to them, in ways that allow for the power differentials to be addressed?

- How do we think about power in the spaces we create? The issues are not just to do with who is in the collective but also the dynamics within the collective itself. Who has a voice? Who has to struggle to be heard? Who has power and who does not?

- How do we create cross-class/race/sexualities solidarities that address issues of power? And use them to our advantage?

- How do we build on what we each have to offer – on our strengths – in a way that ensures "power with" not "power over"?

- How do we ensure inclusion? If you are comfortable there is something you are not seeing and so we have to continually interrogate our location: Who is and who is not in the room? Whose voice is being heard?

- What tools do we need to find/create in order to map the new and rapidly changing geographies of power that we want to challenge and confront?

- How do we take the redistribution of all kinds of resources or geographic segregation seriously?

- How do we keep the energy, convince funders/comrades how important process is as struggles of this nature take time and emotional commitment?

- How do we value individuals and groups within processes that are long and difficult/complex?

- How do we hang on and remain a thriving collective when the pressures from outside, and indeed inside the self, pull in altogether different directions?

5. SEEKING A REVOLUTIONARY PERSPECTIVE

Simply "adding" new concerns like water, or housing, to existing feminist agendas, without letting those new questions and concerns upset and reorganise the agendas, is insufficient. How then do we balance our immediate needs like houses, land, electricity, water, healthcare – which are the things we need to have in order to live – with ensuring that even as we pursue our immediate basic human needs, we do not lose sight of the need to transform the structural organisation of power in society and the world that dictates that majorities of people are oppressed and exploited?

With this approach we are not giving starving women fish, or even teaching them how to fish, we are changing the choice, the terms and the value of fishing so that those who come after us have greater choice and agency. This is hard to do precisely because the parallel systems of neoliberal capitalism and patriarchy reduce us to day-to-day survival, unleashing brute force when we resist: dividing our movements, killing our leaders, starving us, calling us impatient and unreasonable.

To put it another way, Ronald described this dilemma as a struggle to "fight for reforms while arguing for revolution … what I've been trying to figure out, is how do you not … just become defined by struggles for reforms, because all of these struggles are good in and of themselves. It's a good thing that people in Mitchell's Plain get water and people in Khayelitsha get electricity and people in Delft get houses and outsourced workers at UCT decent wages, but that is not in itself revolutionary. It is not going to change the system. So how do you then support these struggles for reforms but not support reformism but encourage people to become revolutionaries and if you do, do you actually enhance the strength for the struggle for reforms or do you diminish it?"

For lasting emancipation, we have to make visible and fight the systemic issues of capitalism and patriarchy. Shereen described one way to do this: "UCT workers are fighting for better salaries and working conditions, on return to their homes, they are fighting for access to electricity or water or healthcare or or or ... Silo struggles are important, but not enough, because it's about more fundamental change. The start of it is to do the work of what I call joining the dots, that will allow the dots between the household and the workspace and all the other spaces in which we conduct our work-home-life to be linked." UCT workers then, joining the dots, allow us to see that we may be striking for a pay increase of R3,500 today or a pay increase of 7.5% but in a year's time R3,500 will not be enough. So we will take to the street, striking for 7.5% again – we need to stop and think what exactly a 7.5% pay increase is? R262? Instead we need to be asking for a decent wage. What is a decent wage in the current context?

We need to change the way collective bargaining and salaries are determined. We have to fight tooth and nail just to force farmowners to pay the newly established minimum wage, which is still too little to live off. We continue to fight farmdweller evictions – but we cannot claim freedom if in those reclaimed homes, women are still being beaten, gay and lesbian teenagers still shunned, and children continue to be born with foetal alcohol syndrome, suffering the effects of systemic poverty and the abusive apartheid tot system of being paid in alcohol. Feminist political education and women-only spaces can begin to do the difficult work of connecting these dots, work which Virginia noted was critical: "Culture and socialisation play a big role in how women think and behave, amongst themselves and amongst men. … We need to try to draw a line between culture and women's rights. It's difficult, but it needs to be done."

A part of this revolutionary perspective must include unlearning what we have been socialised to believe. This is not about replacing one one-sided worldview with another. It is not about tearing down and critiquing the dominant system and then planting nice ready-made answers about the clear alternative into our emptiness. No. It's about unlearning one-sidedness altogether and becoming comfortable with multiple realities, with uncertainty, with openness. It is not about unlearning the information content of one specific paradigm or lesson but about engaging in a process of becoming active learners, prepared to always question our assumptions, to take ownership of our own learning and decide on the principles we wish to learn by. In this approach the process/means is as important as the product/end. There is no one alternative to the dominant system. There is a multiplicity of them that need to be appropriate to different contexts. We will only discover these alternatives through asking questions and taking risks, through doing the work, running many small diverse experiments, making mistakes, learning from each other, and listening to our knowledge and our intuition.

QUESTIONS

- How do we create the spaces of freedom for the experimentation and openness that is needed?
- How do we push for reforms without falling into reformism?

- How do we work with women where they are and address their immediate needs like transport, childcare, food whilst fighting for that situation to change?
- How do we insist on connecting the dots, on measuring freedom by our own standards?

6. DEVELOPING A NEW LANGUAGE

To connect the dots, to not just feel but see how our oppression is linked, how patriarchy works, we need a new language, words, concepts that describe what we experience, as opposed to ones that divide our struggles from private/public, work/home, etc. We need our voices heard. A part of the personal is political is insisting on being seen and heard as a whole person and it is no surprise that the words for this do not exist.

All our categories of thought, all our assumptions about what is reality, or what is politics or economics or even where we live, are so permeated by power that often our language, the means by which we explain the world to ourselves, is limiting and inadequate. But in challenging this we have to do more than simply reproduce the words that already exist. It requires us to create our own words and ways of naming which will allow us to not only be aware but claim and resist our reality in order to fight for our own emancipation. Naming is a vehicle to action.

Language has the power to influence our perceptions and structure our world view. The stigma created by offensive phrases or epithets can be challenged with the empowerment that comes from taking control of language. Try and ask anyone what patriarchy or feminism is in isiXhosa or isiZulu. The way we talk about ourselves and what is appropriate language to do this is a strong way to encourage others to adapt to changing times. And when we do develop a political language that serves our own purpose, we have to guard it or reclaim it because the potential for our words to get depoliticised through an uptake into the mainstream is a very real and ever-present possibility.

QUESTIONS

- How do we think about and use language?
- How do we work across different languages?
- How do we create dialogues to put words to our experiences?
- How do we create new and collective understandings in different languages including poetry, music and print and electronic media?
- How can we monitor the use of language and meaning by powerful institutions?
- How do we argue for or against the processes that make our concerns invisible or unimportant?

7.   ALTERNATIVE INSTITUTIONS

We need to be free to dream and imagine alternative institutions for change. As Koni explained: "There are alternative spaces to have conversations but are there alternative institutions and structures to do for you what the family, legal system, educational system, churches, medical system do? We are critical of them [mainstream institutions] but also stuck in them. So it's about setting up alternative structures and ways of relating."

How can our feminist principles inform and infuse how we relate through all our organisational forms across the private/public divide, in such a manner that people are not treated as objects or used as instruments to some end? Sipho argued: "I must never lose sight of the questions: how is this affecting women? Who is this struggle marginalising? What are we not seeing? How are we contributing to the very problems we are trying to address? … We also need new ways as some of our formulas are simply perpetuating the conditions we attempt to transform."

So we need different models of leadership. As Ronald observed: "It's a big temptation in all groups of oppressed people to say we are too busy or don't have the skills to run the organisation collectively and not undermine each others' capacity to make decisions for ourselves, so let's just leave this to smaller groups who have the time and energy and skills and that may bring a small improvement, decisions happen and things move, but in the long term the capacity of the membership to keep control over themselves and their organisation diminishes as the confidence and power of the leadership grows, which feeds into the possibility of that leadership becoming a self-serving elite. So even if it means going slower don't ever postpone the task of creating a movement that actually reflects the society that you want."

If we move beyond our organising work we also need examples of different ways of being and relating. People need to come together in communities and in the workplace to make decisions about their own lives, instead of decisions about governance, community life and the economy being made by corporations, government bodies, or those with the power and privilege to seize authority. Some principles that we could draw upon include: forms of direct democracy that allow each individual to undertake the necessary research and have input regarding decisions that affect their life and then engaging in decision-making processes that optimise participation and allow for a decision that is acceptable to everyone; the belief in community and sharing; tasks, whatever they may be, are rotated and no skill, position, gender, ethnicity, job or religion has more power or status than any other; underpinnings of reciprocity, communalism, free association, mutual aid and the pooling of resources; attempts to eradicate all forms of domination, such as capitalism, sexism, racism and homophobia. People have the right to participate in decisions that affect their lives.

In creating the laboratory to experiment with alternative institutions and ways of being we are reminded of Arundhati Roy's dictum: "To love. To be loved. To never forget your own insignificance. To never get used to the unspeakable violence and the vulgar disparity of life around you. To seek joy in the saddest places. To pursue beauty to its lair. To never simplify what is complicated or complicate what is simple. To respect strength, never power. Above all, to watch. To try and understand. To never look away. And never, never, to forget."

QUESTIONS

- Who sets the agenda?
- Who decides what spaces can and cannot exist?
- Where are the meetings held? When?
- How can we work differently?
- How do you show or share power and authority?
- Is the organisational form serving the interests of our struggle?
- What would collective leadership look like? What would a different model of leadership look like?

- What kind of trust is possible? What kinds of relationships are possible? What kind of community is possible?
- How do we use feminist principles to inform our roles as parents, partners, workers, etc?

8.   WELL-BEING

In the busyness of our feminist activist lives, we often consider ourselves less and less. As women we need to prioritise our well-being. Without taking the time to do this we continue to rob ourselves of our right to live in balance. The neoliberal patriarchal context in which we live and organise takes away our own sense of power and control over our lives and this is characterised by brutalities of many different forms. These intensities play out across our bodies and psyches. Capitalist patriarchy leads us to believe that self-care is the preserve of the middle and upper classes, instilling attitudes of martyrdom and destructive self-sacrifice among those who identify with radical working-class struggles.

QUESTIONS

- When did you last take time out for yourself – to read, sit, visit with friends, take a walk in nature or do whatever best nurtures your self?
- When did you last have a full medical examination and feel comfortable asking all the questions you have about your body and health?
- What support mechanisms do you have around you? How can you strengthen and build a support base for yourself?

9. VIGILANCE ON VIOLENCE

We know that the price of destabilising power and challenging patriarchy will be violence in some form or another. To continue our activism without arming ourselves to be prepared for violence would constitute a betrayal because patriarchy depends on interpersonal violence for its routine reproduction. The obvious mutually encouraging relationships between patriarchy and violence should inform social activism at every step. Campaigns to eliminate violence that are limited to certain days are good but not enough; they leave key supporting institutions of patriarchy unchallenged. Limiting our understanding of violence to physical violence or extreme acts of brutality is not enough – everyday we live the structural violence of water cut-offs and the like as well as the emotional violence of sexism and discrimination, exclusion and backlash as Virginia pointed out, many women "decide to leave the activist sphere because it is oppressive. It takes a lot of courage. There are too many sites of struggle. Sometimes you find yourself asking the question, "Do I really have to?"' The issue of violence must be brought to the centre of awareness and both individual and collective responses must be prepared collectively. We have to be vigilant and we have to be prepared for violence.

QUESTIONS

- What is our understanding of power and violence?
- How do we uncover interpersonal violence and structural violence in our lives? How do we understand the link between the two? What strategies can we develop to counter these violences?
- How do we incorporate a vigilance on violence in our work?

- How do we think practically about creating and protecting safe spaces, as well as protecting ourselves in the spaces that we occupy on a day-to-day basis?
- How do we protect our gains whilst not becoming protectionist?
- How do we prepare for blacklash whilst going forward, boldly?

BEYOND THESE PAGES

This book has been a conversation between activists and we now invite you, the reader, to be a part of this conversation. Engage with the ideas and the questions, debate them, interrogate them. For the only way change can happen is through dialogue that builds the collective and ultimately supports action. New ways of imagining, relating and working with power in its diverse manifestations and framings have to be crafted now. We believe that this is possible through a new feminist political vision that frames our activism so we can more strategically co-determine transition for our freedom as well as for the freedom of all who are oppressed. This can no longer be postponed.

Endnote

1. Developed and written by Shereen Essof and Koni Benson in consultation with contributing authors.

APPENDIX 1: INTERVIEW TIPS

INTERVIEW QUESTIONS

- What is your name?
- Tell me about the organisation/formation you come from? What is its vision for women?
- How have the socio-economic and political developments informed this work-life-organising?
- What have been the highlights/successes of your work?
- What have been the disappointments/weaknesses?
- What are the key lessons in moving forward?

1. You will be conducting interviews in groups of three with a scribe to record the interview.
2. Decide in your group beforehand who is to be interviewed first, second, third and who will be asking the questions.
3. Maintain eye contact with the person you are interviewing as much as possible.
4. Listen carefully and establish a relaxed style of questioning.
5. Allow the questions to flow.
6. Be open to new questions and new points raised during the interview. Make a note of things raised that you would want to follow up on with further questions.
7. Observe non-verbal behaviour; make sure the person being interviewed is comfortable.
8. Each interview should last 30 minutes; make sure that you observe time.
9. Thank the person being interviewed for their time and sharing.

APPENDIX 2: SOME GUIDELINES FOR EDITING YOUR TRANSCRIPT

1. Read through the draft transcript.

2. When you come across a line or paragraph that you feel needs work, make a brief note in the margin and continue.

3. In the first read-through don't dwell on little details as this will bog you down. Later, you can make the necessary changes directly into the document.

4. After your first read, are you satisfied with your interview?

5. Substantive editing can now begin.

6. Go back over the notes you made in the margins during the first read-through and make the necessary adjustments to the substantive parts of your manuscript. This may include the following:

    *   very small changes to words
    *   rephrasing/or rewriting sections as long as those changes are improvements
    *   deleting sections
    *   explaining further and making points clearer.

7. Once you are done with this substantive editing process and you are happy with the changes/edits you have made, read through the entire document again.

8. Your manuscript is now close to completion. Are you happy with it?

Glossary

Agency

The capacity of individuals to act independently and to make their own free choices. This is sometimes hindered or restricted by certain forces or structures like social class, religion, gender, ethnicity, custom, etc, which can limit or influence the opportunities that individuals have to act.

Agendas

Announced or unannounced objectives, needs, expectations, or strategies of a person or group when participating in an activity.

Anti-capitalist

Taking a stand against capitalism. This includes a wide variety of movements, ideas, and attitudes which oppose capitalism. Anti-capitalists, in the strict sense of the word, are those who wish to replace capitalism with another system.

Anti-essentialist

Taking a stand against essentialism. Essentialism is the philosophical notion that every phenomenon can be broken down into primary, inalterable properties – essences – which determine its nature; if these essences are fully understood, then the phenomenon will be fully understood. However, description and knowledge are socially constructed, and therefore flexible, and conceptualised in terms informed by theory. Essentialism results in the view that females (or males) have an essential nature (e.g. nurturing and caring versus being aggressive and selfish), as opposed to differing by a variety of accidental or contingent features brought about by social forces.

Anti-homophobic

Taking a stand against homophobia (the fear and hatred of homosexuality).

Anti-racist

Taking a stand against racism.

Anti-sexist

Taking a stand against sexism.

Autonomous

Not controlled by others or by outside forces, independent, self-directed.

Autonomy

A self-governing state, community or group.

Bourgeois authoritarianism

Authoritarianism refers to the principle of submission to authority. Bourgeois authoritarianism refers to the principle of submission to those authorities established and needed by modern bourgeois or capitalist societies, for example the authority of property owners, corporate managers, state officials and politicians.

Capitalism

Either an economic system based on private ownership of capital or a social system organised around this type of economic system. Capital can be seen as wealth in the form of money or property owned by a person or business and human resources of economic value, all used to generate more capital.

Chauvinist

Attitudes and behaviours of superiority towards someone of another gender.

Citizens

Residents of a city, town or country, especially those with the entitlement to vote and enjoy other privileges.

Collective

Done by or characteristic of individuals acting together.

Commodify

To to transform goods and services (or things that may not normally be regarded as goods or services) into a commodity (something that is bought and sold).

Corrective rape

A criminal practice, whereby men rape lesbian women, purportedly as a means of "curing" women of their sexual orientation. Most reports of corrective rape originate from South Africa.

Deconstruction

An idea that meaning is constructed. Deconstruction includes discovering and understanding the underlying assumptions, frameworks and ideas that form the foundations for thoughts and beliefs.

Depoliticise

To remove the political aspect from, or remove from political control or influence.

Devaluing

To remove the value from something or deprive a thing of value.

Dichotomy

Division into two contradictory parts or opinions.

Discourse

Expression in speech or writing; the use of a particular kind of political language.

Emancipation

The act or process of setting free, often used to describe various efforts to obtain political rights or equality for a marginalised group.

Femininities

Refer to qualities and behaviours judged by a particular culture as ideally associated with or especially appropriate to women. A feminine woman may have physical attributes different from those of a masculine male. These are often associated with personality traits such as nurturing, life-giving qualities, creativity, and openness, or yielding, to other people.

Feminisation of labour

The expansion of trade, capital flows and technological advances have resulted in the feminisation of labour as more and more women leave their traditional roles as mothers and homemakers to fill new job openings introduced by globalisation. Gender discrimination, violence, sweatshops and sexual harassment are some of the adverse results of the global effects of feminisation of labour. As the global economy expands, multinational companies are looking everywhere to recruit women, both in the developing and the developed world, because women have historically worked for lower wages and have been seen as less likely to organise. Therefore, women are expected to work for low wages, no job security and no autonomy.

Feminism

The understanding that women's oppression is rooted in a system of patriarchy and that this system and its inherent powers need to be challenged and overthrown in order to achieve freedom for women and all people. Under the rubric of feminism there are many different theories, strategies and approaches, and as such many different types of feminists.

Gender identity

The gender(s) a person self-identifies as, or the way other people identify the person's gender, or a combination of the two; not necessarily based on biological fact, either real or perceived, nor is it always based on sexual orientation. The gender identities one may choose from include: male, female, both, somewhere in between, a third gender or neither.

Gender relations

Relations between men and women, both in terms of how we think women and men should behave, and in material terms of who has what resources. Gender is not determined biologically, as a result of sexual characteristics of either women or men, but is constructed socially. It is a central organising principle of societies, and often governs the processes of production and reproduction, consumption and distribution

Glass ceiling

An unacknowledged barrier that prevents women and other oppressed groups from rising to positions of power or responsibility within any kind of organisation. It is invisible until you bump into it.

Hetero-normative

The assumption that being straight and growing up and joining nuclear heterosexual families is the norm; anything that strays from or threatens this model is considered odd, bad, unnatural and dangerous to the individual and society as a whole.

Heterosexual

Attraction to the opposite sex; someone who is straight, not gay.

Homophobic

Fear of homosexuals and of homosexuality; a negative attitude to same-sex relationships and to those who engage in them. Homophobia is sexist because it discriminates on the basis of very narrowly defined roles and options for being male or female.

Ideologies

Mindsets, ideas, or beliefs that form the basis of a political, economic, or social system.

Imperialism

The extension or imposition of power, authority, or influence; the policy, practice, or advocacy of extending the power and dominion of a nation, especially by direct territorial acquisitions or by gaining indirect control over the political or economic life of other areas, countries or regions.

Interpersonal violence

Violence between individuals.

Knowledge production

The dynamics and context of producing information and ideas. This act or work is not neutral or god-given, but political and created by people under a specific set of circumstances, which plays an important role in what we end up labelling as information/facts/knowledge, etc.

Liberal capitalist democracy

A democratic regime based on the recognition of the following: 1) individual rights and freedoms; 2) the rule of law; 3) the separation of state power into a legislative branch (parliament), a judiciary (the court) and an executive branch (government); and 4) a capitalist economy. Such a society is dominated by an elite consisting of the most powerful leaders of the state and the richest owners and top managers of the economy. The working class is an oppressed class in a liberal capitalist democracy.

Liberal feminism

A type of feminism that seeks the equality of men and women through political and legal reform within the confines of a liberal, capitalist democracy.

Mainstreaming

A process of consistently incorporating a sensitivity of gender differences in policy, planning, budgeting, and implementation of programmes and projects in order to overcome inequalities between men and women, boys and girls. The underlying idea is often that existing institutions are not obstacles to women's liberation if they are made sensitive to gender differences.

Masculinities

The characteristics seen as appropriate to the male sex; qualities traditionally ascribed to men, which differ in different times and places. Typically, these involve characteristics such as strength and boldness and are constructed in opposition to traditional feminine characteristics, such as weakness and softness, and are projected as superior to anyone – female or male – who does not embody these characteristics. Exposing the way in which these categories are made up by society rather than predetermined by one's physical sex, or "essentialised" by the body one is born into, or crossing the traditional male/female divide, often results in violence.

Militarism

An ideology which claims that the military is the foundation of a society's security and thereby claims to be its most important aspect. Sexist behaviour and values associated with the military are therefore promoted and celebrated.

Misogyny

Hatred of women.

Nationalism

Refers to an ideology, a sentiment, a form of culture, or a social movement that focuses on the nation. Its goal is to establish, take over, empower and enrich a particular nation state at the expense of oppressing non-members. It usually has a distinct vision of the ethnic identity and political behaviour that is proper for the members of the nation. Nationalism also means love of country and willingness to sacrifice for it, and the belief that nations will benefit from acting independently rather than collectively, emphasising national rather than international goals, and wanting national independence from dominating countries. Critics argue that a main characteristic of nationalism is to invent a past that suits the current needs and goals of the people in power.

Neoliberalism

A political orientation originating in the 1960s, neoliberalism espouses economic liberalism as a means of promoting economic development. Economic liberalism means governments are to prioritise creating the best conditions for secure, profitable investment by big businesses. It promotes the policies of privatisation, austerity, and trade liberalisation dictated to dependent countries by the International Monetary Fund and the World Bank as a condition for approval of investment, loans, and debt relief.

Norms

A standard, model or pattern regarded as typical or "normal"; the spoken and unspoken rules used by a group for appropriate and inappropriate values, beliefs, attitudes and behaviours. Failure to conform to these norms or follow the rules can result in severe punishments. Examples are: only women, not men, wear dresses; or the current middle-class norm of two children per family.

Organisational forms

Ways of structuring the boundaries, roles, and relationships of a group. Organisational forms define how the institution will run, including the roles and relationships, and considers hierarchies, power, division and control of labour, and objectives of the group beyond its current individual members.

Orientation – political or sexual

The direction of one's interests. This can be used to describe political orientation or sexual orientation – where are you facing, what are you drawn towards? Where do you position yourself? If one is lost or looking for something, you use a set of references, or what you are familiar with and drawn to, to orient yourself and determine your bearings, physically or intellectually. As with a compass or a map, there is a shared context, but many options or points along a continuum with which one can identify/place oneself.

Othering

Difference and distancing to prop up one's own ego/superiority through an illusion that the other is inferior. Othering is a way of defining and securing positive identities through the stigmatisation of an "other". Whatever the markers of social differentiation that shape the meaning of "us" and "them" – whether based on race, sexual orientation, gender, geographic, ethnic, economic or ideological differences – there is always the danger that these markers will become the basis for a self-affirmation that depends upon the denigration of the other group. Othering lays the ground for hierarchical and stereotypical thinking and acting.

Outsourcing

Delegating or shifting a part or all of the company's daily operations or business to an external business provider in order to cut costs. If these services are performed by people who are not full-time employees the company saves money by cutting the hours/salaries of workers.

Patriarchy

A social system in which the father is the head of the clan or family (the patriarch), descent follows a male line and men have authority over women and children; a family, community, or society based on this system or governed by men. Patriarchy uses many institutions/ relationships to perpetuate this system of exploitation: sexuality, the household, male-on-female and male-on-male violence, paid employment, cultural and religious and legal and educational institutions, and the state. Patriarichy results in control by men of a disproportionately large share of power.

Personal is political

An idea that came out of the 1960s/70s women's movement, which rejected the separation between public and private life traditionally ascribed to men and women and their roles in society. According to this view, there is no divide between personal relations and the more public world of work and politics. This means that women's problems are not their individual problems to solve, but often a result of unequal power dynamics and can be solved through political change.

Polarisation

To focus on two conflicting or contrasting positions; to explain something in black and white terms, as if there were no grey in between or other possibilities – as if they were "polar opposites" like the two ends of the earth – North and South Pole.

Political paradigms

Frameworks of political thinking that include a set of assumptions, concepts, values, and practices constituting a way of viewing reality for the community that shares these.

Positioning

Where something is placed, including a perspective, or a social rank. This may shift depending on who or what else is around and exerting influence.

Power over

A power relation that is unjust and oppressive to those over whom power is exercised. Domination is a term that can be used for unjust or oppressive "power over" relations. A significant strand of feminist theorising of power starts with the theory that the conception of power as "power over", domination or control is implicitly masculinist.

Power to

Many feminists from a variety of theoretical backgrounds have argued for a reconceptuali-sation of power as a capacity or ability, specifically the capacity to empower or transform oneself and others. Thus, these feminists have tended to understand power not as power over but as power to.

Public and private

Public issues are seen as those that concern society as a whole or a cross section thereof. These issues are understood to be open to public discussion and political intervention. Private issues are seen as the business of the individual and whomever that person wants to involve. It is not considered proper to discuss these things in public. The distinction between public and private issues is generally used to justify the oppression of women as private "family" matters.

Queer

Any sort of sexual orientation that differs from the "norm" of heterosexuality.

Quotas

A proportional share assigned to a group or to each member of a group; a number or percentage, especially of people, constituting a required or targeted minimum.

Radical feminism

A current within feminism which focuses on the theory of patriarchy as a system of power that organises society into a complex of relationships based on an analysis of male supremacy used to oppress women. Radical feminism aims to challenge and overthrow patriarchy and calls for a radical reordering of society.

Racism

A belief that race is the primary determinant of human traits and capacities and that racial differences produce an inherent superiority of one race over another.

Radicalism

A political and/or social movement and ideologies that aim at fundamental change in the structure of society.

Regenerate

To form, construct, or create anew, especially in an improved state; to give new life or energy.

Reproduction

The sexual process by which organisms generate new individuals of the same kind; procreation.

Reproductive roles

Interactions between biological make up and social settings assign people certain roles in the conception, gestation (pregnancy), nurturing and care of human beings. Women are assigned most of the work of performing these reproductive roles. To a very large extent, this is both a cause and consequence of sexist discrimination against women, as men claim social power, wealth and leisure for themselves while women are expected to bear children and care for them (and their fathers, uncles and grandfathers).

Sexism

Prejudice or discrimination based on sex, especially discrimination against women. This is supported in many different ways that are key to our socialisation into our sex roles, and therefore makes this domination acceptable in society – through language, visual association, media representation and stereotyping, especially on the basis of the maternal/caring role of women. Women experience sexism in different ways within the family and the workplace, depending upon their social and economic situation, and sexism limits the ways in which women can actualise their potential.

Sexual orientation

Refers to a person's preference for a sexual partner of a specific sex.

Sexuality

Sexuality is a central aspect of being human throughout life and encompasses sex, gender identities and roles, sexual orientation, eroticism, pleasure, intimacy and reproduction. Sexuality is experienced and expressed in thoughts, fantasies, desires, beliefs, attitudes, values, behaviours, practices, roles and relationships. While sexuality can include all of these dimensions, not all of them are always experienced or expressed. Sexuality is influenced by the interaction of biological, psychological, social, economic, political, cultural, ethical, legal, historical and religious and spiritual factors .

Situated solidarity

A union of interests, purposes, support among members of a group and a fellowship of responsibilities and interests in a particular place or location.

Socio-economic

Relationship between economic activity and social life.

Socialisation

Learning the customs, attitudes, norms and values of a social group, community, or culture.

Straight

Heterosexual, which refers to men being sexually attracted to women and women to men.

Strategy

Any plan for achieving goals or objectives.

Structural violence

A form of violence which corresponds with the systematic ways in which a social structure or institution destroys people slowly by preventing them from meeting their basic needs. Institutionalised elitism, ethnocentrism, classism, racism, sexism, adultism, nationalism, heterosexism and ageism are some examples of structural violence. Life spans are reduced when people are socially dominated, politically oppressed or economically exploited. Structural violence and direct violence are highly interdependent. Structural violence inevitably produces conflict and, often, direct violence including family violence, racial violence, hate crimes, terrorism, genocide and war.

Subjugation

To bring under control; conquer; to make subservient or enslave.

Submission

Giving up or surrendering to the power of another.

Subordination

To make inferior to another; to place in a lower rank; to lessen in dignity.

Systemic oppression

How one power group dominates another through direct control and pervasive disinformation about race, ethnicity, gender, sexual orientation or any other aspect of the targeted or oppressed group.

Theorise

To formulate or assert as a tentative explanation. Theories are analytical tools for understanding, explaining and making predictions about a given subject matter.

Traditionalism

Adherence to beliefs or customs taught by one generation to the next, often orally; the observance of a set of customs or practices that can be informed by, amongst other things, culture or religion.

Transgress

To go beyond or over (a limit or boundary); exceed or overstep; for example, to act in violation of, a cultural practice or stated law.

Undermine

To lessen or deplete the nerve, energy or strength of someone or something; to damage, destroy, or defeat by sabotage.

Unmasked/Unmasking

To disclose the true character of someone or something.

World Bank

An international financial institution that provides conditional loans to developing countries.

Xenophobic

A person unduly fearful or contemptuous of that which is "foreign", especially strangers or "foreign" peoples.

Index